ABOLITIONIST SOCIALIST FEMINISM

ABOLITIONIST SOCIALIST
FEMINISM
Radicalizing the Next Revolution

ZILLAH EISENSTEIN

MONTHLY REVIEW PRESS
New York

Copyright © 2019 by Zillah Eisenstein
All Rights Reserved

Library of Congress Cataloging-in-Publication Data
available from the publisher.

ISBN cloth: 978-1-58367-762-9

Typeset in Minion Pro and Bliss

MONTHLY REVIEW PRESS, NEW YORK
monthlyreview.org

5 4 3 2 1

For the murdered children of Hiroshima, Syria, Yemen, Palestine and the captured, caged, and homeless children in the U.S.

. . . the old is dying and the new cannot be born.
—ANTONIO GRAMSCI

We revolt simply because, for many reasons,
we can no longer breathe.
—FRANTZ FANON

When I dare to be powerful, to use my strength in
the service of my vision, then it becomes less and less
important whether I am afraid.
—AUDRE LORDE

Today is always yesterday.
—SCRATCHED ON A WALL IN SÃO PAULO, BRAZIL

A FEW FOUNDATIONAL QUERIES

why socialism?

Everyone deserves to live without the fear of hunger and homelessness and illness and unemployment and disability. The profit motive destroys humanity. A start toward socialism would be a universal livable wage and health care for all.

why feminism?

Because neither sex nor gender should determine one's life choices. And because misogyny, the hatred of women, and heteropatriarchy, the structural support for women's inequality, continually seek to control and regulate women's bodies. My use of the term *women* always is inclusive of trans, gender-variant, queer, nonbinary identities. It is a specifically universal embrace.

Feminism must create access and freedom for all of our sexual and reproductive bodies. Reform, as in women's rights, is still threaded and structured through racist heteropatriarchy. So in the spirit of writer Mab Segrest, *queer* all this as well.

why abolitionism?

Chattel slavery has only been reformed, and personhood and civil and human rights remain unfulfilled. White supremacy must be completely uprooted from the structuring law, prisons, and the racist division of labor. Abolition is the totality needed to end the outrageous abuse and obscene everyday punishment of U.S. Blacks and other people of color, trans, queer, and straight alike. Abolition must abolish and not simply reform. Abolitionism is often used today to refer to the robust movement to end the prison system. My usage extends to the structural totality of misogynist racism wherever it thrives.

Why am I still forced to be making this case after all the years of antiracist, antimisogynist critiques of capitalist racist heteropatriarchy? Why is this still the question? Why haven't progressive thinkers and activists of all stripes changed more? Why does the left fail to recognize that the personal *is* political, that there is a politics to sex, that sexualized racism is foundational to class?

Is it this exclusiveness of radical and revolutionary history that explains why there has never been a successful socialist revolution? Is that the reason why revolutions have merely chosen to reform parts of the nexus of power and oppression and exploitation? Is it that socialism needs more heart and body, more abolitionist socialist feminisms?

We—those wishing for revolutionary change—need to move forward. If we remain mired in the old, we will just repeat it.

the challenges that follow

What do you do when socialism is not enough?
You make it antiracist and feminist.

What do you do when feminism is not enough?
You make it socialist and antiracist.

What do you do when antiracism is not enough?
You make it socialist and feminist.

And then what do you do?
You make sure this abolitionist socialist feminism is fully inclusive, most especially of gays and trans and disabled people.

We may be living in a moment of what physicists call "singularity." In political terms, this means that whatever came before has sunk into a metaphorical black hole, making the past indiscernible and the present incomprehensible/untranslatable. I remember thinking this when the election was handed over to George Bush in 2000. It was unprecedented and an early warning sign of what was to come in 2016.

I don't think anyone can get ahead of history and know future possibilities, but I do think you can constrain history and hold it back if you do not have new ways of seeing. State actors believe they are supposed to mystify the power structure, not expose it. It is important to recognize that this so-called protective capacity has shifted. The tension is between an effective state that obfuscates what it is and Trump, who reveals too much: We have a Klan president of sorts, who is also a sexual predator as well as a capitalist apologist. What is happening with this new chaotic exposure? Some might say that fascism has become completely transparent.

I am reminded of what the South African artist William Kentridge writes about post-apartheid South Africa. He says that one of the strangest things is that little has changed. Children in poor rural schools still get a miserable education and the main beneficiaries of the end of apartheid remain white South Africans. Yet he says that his compromised society nurtures and nourishes his work. This makes him *suspicious of certainty*, valuing instead the *provisionality* of the moment. Because of the world he lives in, he values *doubt*. So do I. It keeps me curious and open.

Why is misogyny so seldom named as a structural system of sexual power? And why must I continually return to the misogynist structure of racism and capitalism? Why does misogyny remain silenced and unnamed, an open secret in this moment? It is visibly invisible and naturalized and normalized as such. Is it this that gives patriarchy its incredible resilience, a suppleness that stymies a full-throttle assault?

What is it about capitalism that sucks all of the air out of a buoyant racial and sexual and gender critique? After all, it seems apparent that *in this moment* we need to target the entirety: capitalist heteropatriarchal racism.

Why and how is patriarchal privilege ignored, naturalized, and normalized into a shattering silence? Why are rape and sexual violence not seen as part of the structural privilege underpinning capitalism and racism? How does this silence allow sexual violence to be the glue of racist patriarchal oppression?

Why does class so regularly trump (so to speak) race and gender? Why, when inequality is recognized, is it seen as fundamentally economic and class defined—especially when people of color and white women of the working class remain disproportionately poor and sexually violated?

Why today is white supremacy, even when it is

acknowledged, simply reformed but not abolished? Why does queerness remain the elephant in the room when doing antiracist work?

Why are the issues bifurcated? Race or class? Sex or race? Class or sex? Why not ask how they relate and combine with each other? Why do progressives not wonder more about how multiple interlocking power structures operate simultaneously?

Why, although sexual violence is pervasive to the systems of militarism, capitalism, imperialism, and racism, is it not viewed as being as essential to oppression as capitalism?

How can activists face this urgent moment with defiance and turn our resistance/s and reform actions into revolutionary acts?

Why is it not understood that the most revolutionary and necessary politics for today is a queer abolitionist socialist feminism?

So much has changed. So little has changed. Everything has changed. Not enough has changed. Each is true. What to do?

I. AN INTRO OF SORTS

This writing for this moment is structured as a conversation with you— wherever you are located with your own political consciousness—and myself. I will try to find and expose everything I am thinking so that I build a trust with you. I hope that you will read this and it will help you feel courageously defiant and hopeful. Even if you are not sure about the probability of success, you know that the unbearable suffering in this country and the pain across the planet must be ended. And maybe my offering, my deeply felt intellectual political polemic, will allow you and us to expunge the hate, the exploitation, and cruelty that floods communities across this nation.

I am a white woman who benefits from a structural system of white supremacy and privilege but also suffers its misogynist roots/routes. My imaginings of an abolitionist socialist feminism then demand the uprooting of white supremacy along with an assault on the patriarchal structure that supports both. I will sometimes use *misogynoir,* the term coined by feminist writer Paula Moya, to express this intimate connection between race and gender. And I will continually look for my own complicity in these punishing oppressions.

As I write, I am thinking about my sister friends of color and my love and debt to them. It is this debt, in part, that pushes me to write in these fraught times and say to them that many white people do and can turn against their own privilege, can and do love you even if Trump and his cohorts are working hard to convince you otherwise.

I also write to white women across class divides to say that you should take a stand to abolish the exploitation and hatred that plagues this country and the globe. White antiracist women, and the men they bring with them, young and old, trans and nonbinary, gay, disabled and not, have to become a part of this uprising. Immigrants, people of color, Blacks, LatinX, South Asians are already rising.

My optimism is key to my argument. So, also, is my belief that people are able to change themselves. And that we must catch up with the possibilities that are unraveling today rather than let them pass us by because we do not see the urgency. The massive political and weather calamities displacing and killing millions of us give us no other choice.

I offer my queries as a guide for action and not for simple pondering. Our actions, while forming tenuous connections, will offer new answers yet unknown. I loop through related thoughts and sometimes repeat them so they can be seen in their repetitive formation; I wind and rewind in order to see how race and sex and gender and class protect and expose each other.

I ask you to see my method as illustrative of the incompleteness of political history. In a sense, I mimic the ever-present nature of white misogynist privilege by calling attention to it again and again. Structural inequities recur repeatedly in slightly differing fashion, and not enough critical theory puts this in the bold, allowing us to see the nature of the problems more clearly. If I keep returning to *naming* the problem, I do so to make sure we are readying to see and act. If you get annoyed with this method, think about how the millions suffering oppression feel daily.

My method asks all of us, but especially white people, especially antiracist white women, to open both our eyes and our minds and our language to see deeper into the structures of racist, sexist, and class power. Listen especially carefully to women of color who most often know and have experienced more of the oppression. Most often, the more power you have, the less you know of oppression, the less you see and feel it.

Be ready to engage and risk yourself. Stop wondering

if you are comfortable with change and instead change yourself to wonder how to create fairer and more just lives for the most injured. I am sure of nothing other than *it is time*.

a bit of intro to me

My political history, like most people's, is deeply personal. Our lives are defined by the contexts we inhabit—by the stories we hear and have absorbed and tell—alongside the happenings that are so often not of our own making. I am writing from different coalitional sites that are shifting and changing. My own history pushes me hard to see through to revolutionary actions and alliances for these times.

I grew up in a communist household with my three beloved sisters, Sarah, Giah, and Julia. The civil rights movement defined our lives. Saturday mornings we regularly arose to the call from our parents that it was time to get up and demonstrate. We would get dressed, have breakfast, and leave to join the picket line at places like Woolworth's, where lunch counters were still segregated.

My parents continuously lost their jobs due to redbaiting. We never lived anywhere longer than two years, and always lived in mixed race and Black neighborhoods, which meant we were seen as race traitors by many whites. Our support network was the Black and civil rights community and each other. Today I have seen the language of "comrade," which we always used in our household, shift to "ally" or "accomplice" and wonder about this. Ally or accomplice seem too separate and apart and safe to me. Allies or accomplices support the struggle but are not fully in or of it. For me, I am in it.

In grade school in the 1950s, my schoolmates tormented me and my family for being dirty commie Jews. I pondered how they knew. And since my family was atheist, I wondered what exactly they hated about my Jewishness. Was it just because I easily shared my milk money with others at school? Or because I was the only Jew in North High School in Columbus, Ohio, so it was easy for the bullies to taunt me? This hurt, and I felt alone, but it did not destroy me.

In 2015, when a Black teenage girl was thrown to the ground and manhandled by Texas police at a pool party, I was reminded of the time all those years ago in Columbus when I asked my parents if I could go to a swimming party at a local private pool. They said no, because although the pool was not legally segregated, it was obvious that Blacks were not welcome. I was alone and without friends, and I was angry at them. There were no exceptions or leniencies in my parents' world. You did not ever get to pretend that racism did not matter.

After Dad was denied tenure as part of the red scare at Ohio State University, we moved to Atlanta, Georgia, for what was to be my senior year of high school. Our neighborhood was segregated and Black, except for my family, living in Atlanta University housing. I was so tired of all the upheaval. I knew no one on arrival. I went to Brown High, the newly-so-called integrated white working-class school that was the closest to where I lived. The only Black person at the school was Clemsy Wood. By speaking with him, I isolated myself further.

No one from school would visit my home because it was in the Black neighborhood. When there was a boycott of downtown stores because of their segregated hiring practices, I was not allowed to buy a prom dress, although no one asked me anyway. (A movement friend of my mother's living in New York City sewed one for me and sent it anyhow.)

I had a lead role in the senior play, but my father said he would not attend without family friends, who were Black. As I noted earlier, the school was all white minus one. I asked him not to come and start a race riot, to no avail. Avoidance was not an option when it came to racism. Neither was compromise. My mother was diagnosed with breast cancer the next year. She chose to have her friend, Dr. Asa Yancey, do the surgery, but he was Black so he did not have operating privileges in the local white hospital. She was therefore operated on in the Black hospital. Years later, in my mother's FBI file, I saw that she was identified as Negro. I guess Black hospital meant Negro woman, even if her name was Fannie Price Eisenstein.

By the way, the Barbara Streisand character in the movie *The Way We Were* was based on my mom. She and Arthur Laurents, who wrote the screenplay, were students at Cornell University together. Mom had won a full scholarship; she was otherwise too poor to have attended. Among other activities, she founded the Young Communist League there. Laurents writes that Fannie fascinated him, although my mother would always say that the political activist in the movie was nothing like her. This was true, but we loved teasing her about it anyway.

I went off to college and graduate school and came to full adulthood in the US feminist movement of the 1970s, with Black socialist feminists and lesbians of many colors as my comrades: bell hooks, the sisters Barbara and Beverly Smith, Angela Davis, Hortense Spillers, and Ellen Wade, to name a few.

It was with this antiracist socialist sense of self that I moved through both my early feminist activism and the several decades of activism that followed, when feminism took on more dispersed forms with no organized women's mainstream present. Meanwhile, the feminisms of women of color were percolating and reemerging both here and abroad. I supported Obama against Hillary Clinton in the 2008 primaries, my entrance into electoral activism.

Next came my antiracist feminist activist rebirth in two campaigns initiated by the legal scholar Kim Crenshaw and the African American Policy Forum, which she cofounded. These actions were developed in response to Obama's all-boy initiative, "My Brother's Keeper," and the #SayHerName campaign, which sought to bring to light the police killings of Black women. The interracial camaraderie of this work with Kim and Eve Ensler and journalist Laura Flanders directed me towards an abolitionist socialist feminism.

Then came the painful 2016 election. My socialist self supported Bernie Sanders in the primaries and then reluctantly turned to Hillary Clinton after decades of criticizing her because Trump was so obscene.

This skeletal look at my journey brings me to the present moment, to this book. The repetition of oppression is exhausting and the time for abolitionism is now. Whatever your political persuasion—liberal, leftist, progressive, climate activist, gay, indigenous, disabled, antigun activist, trans, whomever—the time is now.

II. A BEGINNING OF SORTS

What I write here owes itself to more than forty years of dialogue and activism with feminists of every color. These dialogues were embedded in conversations about hundreds of books and articles read and shared, and thousands of actions taken. So this is a collective project for me. As I write, I see and hear the many sister (not cister) friends and colleagues and comrades who have been a part of this conversation.

I am humbled and searching and determined as I continue to write in such troubled times. People are living through political and environmental cyclones. My thoughts are about the feminisms that have improved the way humanity can see this world, live in this world, and change this world.

I try to displace the idea that women as a sex class need a "oneness," a central definition. Today, unlike earlier radical feminism, sex class is to be understood only in terms of its overlapping multiple partialities. So yes, sex class, and raced power, and economic class are each varied and heterogeneous, and this gives them their shared political import.

Complex power systems constitute the overlapping commonness that disallows any oneness, homogeneity, or unity. Instead, ideas of "heterogeneous commonality" and "common differences" that are "differently similar" make up the sexual class of women. I am looking in/at this moment to find new articulations of these complex, overlapping relations of race, sex, class, and genders—between and inside of each. Disabilities and trans identities further illuminate this process.

Why are women's lives more differentiated today *within* the structural systems of patriarchy than in earlier historical periods? Most women across racial lines are working overtime doing the labor necessitated by misogyny *and* they also occupy sites that were once closed to them within this very system of male privilege. But this latter change of females to new sites in the public sphere—presidents, CEOs—has little to do with rearranging structural or collective power.

Women have been or are presidents and secretaries of state and foreign ministers in the United States, Haiti, Liberia, Argentina, Chile, Jamaica, Germany, France, India, Pakistan, and many other countries. Meanwhile, five hundred thousand women die annually in childbirth. And too many millions are displaced, traversing the globe as refugees.

Everything changes and nothing changes. Both of these statements are valid, and with the uncertainty comes new possibility. I am looking for the *new-old* meanings that express both change and stasis. Feminisms are both stuck and have moved beyond languages that are both necessary and outmoded. Should we still use the term *patriarchy* when so much has changed? Why is masculine privilege today more diversely written on women's bodies of all colors and many classes? How can Google still think it is OK to pay women less than men in such obvious discriminatory structural fashion?

Distinctions like first and third world still apply, and they also do not. The third world lives in New York City, and Kentucky Fried Chicken operates in Kenya. The second world disappeared along with the Soviet Union in the revolutions of 1989. Indigenous feminisms are constructed within settler and imperial locations and stand against western imperial feminisms of all sorts.

Female bodies, whatever cultural and racial and class form they take, are a location of both power and powerlessness. If women are bound and gagged, it is because they have potential power. Women will be beaten or raped or mutilated because of this potential power. If one could, one would just ask any enslaved Black female about her body and her punishment, about her power and her powerlessness as a piece of property.

If women's bodies were not sites of power, they would not be the battleground that they are. Sometimes this struggle to control is individual and personal through a sexual violation that is silenced and shamed. And sometimes the struggle is more public, as in the fight over the legal status of abortion, since abortion is a proxy for controlling women's bodies.

The struggle over the legal standing of abortion stymied the unification negotiations between East and West Germany in 1990. West Germany was initially unwilling to accept the more radical abortion laws of the East. Abortion in the United States remained unresolved in the battles over the Obama health care reform. Reproductive rights and self-determination of one's female body are central to all the newest reformations of misogyny—in the United States, in Poland, and in South America, for example. They remain central to the struggle for control of the US Supreme Court.

So female bodies share a homogenous standing in misogyny, while they are also varied in relation to systems of power. On the one hand, there are Hillary Clinton, former secretary of state Condoleezza Rice, former president Ellen Johnson Sirleaf of Liberia, Prime Minister Theresa May of the UK, Chancellor Angela Merkel of

Germany, female defense ministers in Spain and France, and female soldiers at Abu Ghraib.

On the other hand, there are poor migrant women laborers, female flower growers in Honduras, mutilated girls and women in Rwanda, indigenous women protecting land rights throughout the globe, Black women and their children suffering the greatest effects of Hurricanes Katrina, Harvey, and Irma, detained women immigrants in the United States, raped Rohingya women in Myanmar, women of #MeToo.

This disjuncture of power among women is why US antiracist socialist feminists took part in the International Women's Strike of 2017, calling for a feminism of the 99 percent. It was time to come together with restaurant workers, Wal-Mart employees, domestic workers, immigrant women, Black women, and many others. Some of us wear veils, others reveal their faces; some are tattooed, others not; some are trans, some are indigenous, some are gay, others are disabled. Some are made of many of these multiple parts.

As I rethink and update all the changes that are within my purview, I offer an abolitionist socialist feminism as a possible organizing site for the audaciousness already at hand. I am uneasy and doubtful but also equally passionate that radically progressive people —the big "we"—can transform the world, especially with girls and women of color offering leadership around the globe. And because a revolutionary imagination is the most meaningful thing "we" have to offer, let us all try to find it.

III. AFTER TRUMP'S VICTORY

This is a historical moment in need of a bit of theory, meaning connecting the dots between disparate actions in order to see the linkages and see each other. The resistance is mixed and intersectional and wildly chaotic but in a productive way. Yet it has gotten ahead of its theory. Terms like left, liberal, radical, feminist, progressive, are in motion and disassembling. And terms describing Trump, such as protofascist or prefascist or totalitarian, are not nuanced enough to name, and therefore see, the misogynist racist excesses of this regime.

The day after the inauguration there was the spectacular outpouring of resistance by millions in the Women's March on Washington and its sister actions, a mammoth mass demonstration against Trump on the streets of cities and towns across the globe. The marches were mixed racially, even if still predominantly white. And women of color led many of them.

I am ready to recognize the importance of learning

from this amazingly successful action. If it was not radical or revolutionary enough for some, it still offers a fertile site for further radicalization. So what is there important to say about these marches that followed Trump's election, if you forget the hacks and voter suppression and three million more votes for Clinton.

The right wing of this country is *not* the majority. The alt-right, although it garners a lot of visibility, is a small minority, though a frightening one, armed with guns. Their racist and sexist assaults against civility have invigorated and mobilized large numbers of people. As Trump tries to keep his true believers, his so-called *base,* happy, he potentially energizes everyone else.

The rest of the people that Trump loves to hate—taxi drivers, restaurant workers, nurses, women of all colors and classes, the new working class, immigrants, undocumented students throughout the academy, Muslims, Black Lives Matter, Showing Up for Racial Justice, Planned Parenthood, Jewish Voice for Peace, Black Women's Blueprint, Movement of Movements, Standing Rock, the American Civil Liberties Union—are all resisting. There are many more of *us* occupying, protecting, rising, overcoming, resisting, trying to be ungovernable, than there are of them.

Women and men, trans, white and other colors, abled and disabled, the bigger "we" that Trump insists on punishing and excluding, have taken to the streets at every opportunity to build a resistance in the hopes of desta-bilizing his regime. Many have refused to normalize the orderliness of Trump's administration and continually highlight the misogynist and racist commitments made by him and his appointees.

Yet how to see and name this particular political moment? The Electoral College, a leftover of slave-state privileged interests, parades as a democratic safeguard. Instead, it inhibits the voices of the most aggrieved. The two-party system that is supposedly essential to demo-cratic choice, offers little and instead creates gridlock and dysfunction. This dysfunction is used to justify neoliber-al restructuring and downsizing *and* yet nurtures rebel-lion at the same time. Maybe this is the *singular* moment that inadvertently exposes both the function and dys-function of white supremacy in capitalist patriarchy. It is not unimportant that Trump follows our first Black president, even if Obama was no radical on racial issues.

In this critical time, Trump and his regime attempt to prop up *misogynoir* for the ailing capitalism they love so dearly. They cling to a misogyny that emboldens white supremacy, oblivious to its anachronisms and violence. Trump uses multiple hatreds and animus, thinking he can bulldoze an economic recovery into being. He bel-lows forth a cacophonous call to arms. I hope that he will assist in his own destruction. But this cannot happen on its own. It is crucial that the resistance stay simultaneously mobilized and disruptive, multipurposed and unified.

Trump speedily executed executive orders and decrees when he came into office, reinstating the global gag rule, disallowing even the mention of abortion to all the women of color across the globe, supporting settler colonialism by reissuing access rights to the Dakota Access and Keystone Pipelines, making full-blown enemies where they did not previously exist of immigrants and refugees, especially those from Muslim countries.

Huge acts of resistance filled airports throughout the country as Muslim travelers were detained and refused entry. Mass protests greeted Trump's disavowal and dismembering of DACA (Deferred Action for Childhood Arrivals). As well, his anti-immigration zero tolerance policy, separating and detaining young children from their parents, mobilized new segments of activists.

A majority of whites did not support the thuggery of Charlottesville, although Trump did. Trump tweeted that football players who #TakeAKnee should be fired. He called them sons of bitches. He then antagonized not only the NFL, but the NBA also, condemning as unpatriotic anyone who did not stand for the national anthem and the flag.

Colin Kaepernick took a knee to make a statement against police brutality and racist injustice. Trump insisted that his own remarks had nothing to do with racism and were about patriotism. It is lost on Trump that the anthem, the nation, and patriotism are mired in a history of racism.

At this point, more and more players are kneeling with Kaepernick and speaking out against Trump. I am hoping that the mobilization continues even though team owners will be fined if players do not stand for the anthem. I also hope that a more sustained critique of structural racism will develop further. And back to the mothers who Trump says are the bitches. Yet the NFL is mired in numerous allegations of domestic abuse by its players, and the physical brutality of the sport with its horrific head injuries is hardly a location of people's liberation. Nevertheless, there are important sites of resistance from within.

How can these reform movements become revolutionary? Is it possible that because the problem of racist heteropatriarchal capitalism is interlocking, assaults aimed at a single site can disarm and weaken the entire foundation? There may not be a woman president at present, but there are many women leading the resistance in its many forms. Much of the radicalization surrounding electoral politics can morph into unknowable achievements, as demonstrated in the 2018 midterm elections.

If focusing on a part may destabilize the whole, this may mean that the relationship between reform and revolution is redefined as more of an integral process rather than separate and in contradiction. If there is not a single mode of production to attack, but multiple sites that protect the interlocking structure of racist capitalist patriarchy, do reformist politics become a revolutionary possibility? Contemplate with me the demands for single-payer health care, an end to racist policing, and full access to abortion, contraception, and reproductive justice, and imagine how they might help move along the revolutionary process that has already begun.

New questions that need to guide the work are: Is capital so malleable that it is able to absorb modernized systems of gendered racism? Is misogyny so malleable that it can still oppress most women while allowing others to hold positions of power? Can white supremacist capitalist patriarchy withstand substantial racial redefinition and still deliver the necessary exploitative systems? Can white supremacy have Black men and women ruling? The massively popular film *Black Panther* comes to mind. Can Blacks rule a Wakanda in the *real* world? Can Black women warriors bring the peace that we wish for or will the powers that be regroup to prevent such a world?

Capitalism needs more than an update. It needs more than a modernization that would bring multiple and diverse people to positions of power. Rather, it needs every kind of reform leading to and demanding revolution.

Because the problem abolitionists face is complex and multiple, questions that center on capitalism and sideline its white privilege and misogyny are, more than ever, insufficient. The predator-in-chief has made clear for all to see that misogyny (he will grab our pussies if he wants to) and whiteness (his base is white and he will throw everyone else under the bus) are key to saving capitalism.

Just maybe, global capitalist greed is undermining its golden rule. Instead of protecting and occluding the racist heteropatriarchal underbelly of capitalism, Trump upends it by exposing the usually well-kept secret that capital couldn't do much of what it does if it didn't use patriarchy and its deep roots/routes of modernized settler colonialism and chattel slavery to garner its profits.

So it is no surprise that Trump claims to defend white working-class men and promises them their jobs back. But it continues to amaze me that this is never described as *identity politics*. The putdown of *identity politics* is usually reserved for people of color and white women. Only those who criticize the racist, sexist, heterogendered, able-bodied, unfair structuring of citizenship and political life are categorized as indulging in identity politics.

But those of us critiquing the system are paving a new path. Audre Lorde pointed to the master's tools and the master's house, suggesting that they cannot resolve our dilemmas. Rosa Luxemburg understood that revolution cannot be bounded by limited imagination. Let some of us in the resistance call out the failed two-party system. Let many wonder about a third party if they must. Let some call for an end to nationalism and US exceptionalism and the wars necessitated by it. Let others demand an end to climate catastrophe and the destruction of the planet. Let still others imagine a whole new structural apparatus for communities living in a borderless global world.

Following Audre and Rosa, abolitionists need to dream beyond what feels like possibility. We need to mobilize our different movements of many distinct voices into a risk-taking set of coordinated actions. It is for those of us, especially privileged white people, to listen carefully and put our bodies on the line wherever they are needed, between the police and their militarized actions, and alongside our brothers and sisters of color in everyday life.

So feminists need to be and can be simultaneously diverse and unified and multipronged in our visions. Alicia Garza of Black Lives Matter says that the time to act is now, so embrace whoever is ready in this moment. Those of us who are antiracist can unite for the planet and our bodies against Trumpism and its cabal of violators and predators. S/exploitation is key to this system and must be destroyed along with its racial practice of domi/nation.

There are new possibilities to resist, as global capital has demanded the mobility of labor, threading many sites of colonial power, from Europe to the United States, creating a new majority/minority white status. Whiteness is exposed as a minority global characteristic more readily than before, now that the once predominantly white United States struggles to live its supremacist lie at home. And now that countries like France and Germany can no longer spin their white majority standing as one and the same with supremacy. White people have always been a minority in Africa, Asia, and South America. This will soon also be true in the United States and Europe, although as the white apartheid rule in South Africa showed, minorities can and do seize power .

It is essential to know and recognize that the right-wing nationalist, fascist, xenophobic, misogynistic take-over—by Trump, Modi, Putin, Erdogan, Assad, Duter-te, and Bolsonaro—is global. Or as Priya Gopal, who writes about colonial and postcolonial literature, says, if the United States had been paying attention in 2014, it would have begun to worry when Modi, a known fascist, won the presidency of India, a country with one-sixth of the world's population. When Trump spoke at the UN, declaring his policy of America First, and encouraging other nations to follow the same tack by making their own nations the priority, none of this would seem to make any sense for global capital. So beware.

It should be no surprise that women of color, especially Black women, voted against Trump in overwhelming numbers. Yet too many white women, across all class lines, did not. It remains to be seen whether the tenuous yet promissory stance and status of white women can be mobilized for abolitionist feminism. There is no way for this to happen without politicizing the racist misogyny of Trump and all these other right-wing regimes.

"We," the big we, need to find our unity while recognizing our fabulous differences. Black Woman's Blueprint asks us to do this. They mobilized women of color for the Women's March by calling forth a specified agenda that included the needs of all women across class and racial lines. Former congressperson Luis Gutierrez did this when he said he would walk in the Women's March with his wife and daughter because he cared about every slight to every human right.

This political moment can mobilize a new collaboration and a new solidarity that initiates a new revolutionary movement. We, the resistance, must be inside and outside, focus on both the legal and extralegal, be uncompromising and compromising and supportive and embracing of each other. Difference and conflict must be acknowledged and not feared in order for this new movement to grow.

Voices of critique from women of color are opportunities, not condemnations. At moments, demands will be specific and singular. Other times demands will be inclusive. Often the politics will have to be vague and unknown and unsettling.

No one *fully* knows how or why Trump won. No one *really* knows exactly who this elusive white working class is that voted for him. Or why the Democrats undermined Bernie Sanders and chose Hillary Clinton. Nor do we know exactly how the new working classes of women of color across the planet will become the new revolutionary hope. But Ai Jen Poo of the National Domestic Workers Alliance is already hard at work on this: working toward a Domestic Workers Bill of Rights and building liaisons between women workers across the economy.

This moment calls for women of color to go forth and lead the next revolutionary movement. Remember to use what was incredible about your foremother's brilliance and make it better. I am with you, listening and collaborating as more than ally, as an abolitionist sister comrade, freedom fighter, in this struggle to finally upend white supremacy's gendered and capitalist abuse. When *we* are doing the work together, a new world comes forward for each of us.

IV. ON FEMINISMS

Which feminism do I have in mind when I talk about the women's movement? The issue is less whether any individual is or is not feminist, but how can women work together, what kind of a movement can we *all* build so we get to show what we need, and who we are in all our complexity. Of course, the term "we" includes differences of inequalities.

The stakes are really high just now. The world's brutality is unsustainable for the 99 percent. Endless wars along with other climate assaults threaten the air and water and earth and, therefore, *us*. Hillary Clinton's neoliberal feminism has been mainstreamed for decades, and especially during the 2016 election. Feminists of every other sort had little ability to publicize a more inclusive and revolutionary politics. This more revolutionary politics has been in the making for decades, although Hillary was clueless about it.

I like the comment from professor and activist Salamishah Tillet that she wants an "open" but not an "elastic" feminism. And Aysha Hidayattullah, a professor of Islamic Studies at the University of San Francisco, says compellingly that feminism is not a fixed identity but a stance of "radical uncertainty." And I love playwright Eve Ensler's statement about revolution: We are dispersed, but "we know where we are going."

Most borders—among nations, races, genders, sexes, and classes—are disassembling and reconstituting. This is most probably why right-wing activists want to reenforce borders and walls. Many patriarchies remain, but they have changed their form. Now there are many kinds of feminism in response. I am looking to create flux and movement and openness in order to mount a successful assault against the suffering and unhappiness created by the newest systems of racist, heterosexist, ableist, capitalist patriarchy.

In these urgent times of perpetual wars, from Ferguson to Gaza, and the crises of Ebola and Zika that have ravaged countries near and far, insurgent feminisms are more needed than ever. It is impossible to not absorb the sense of danger and risk that threads a never-ending militarism, with the devaluation of human life, most especially Black life. It is a relief to have Beyoncé embrace and expose these unsettled times for and with us. In these detestable moments of Black devaluation, criminalization, and dehumanization, Beyoncé in 2014 responded and popularized feminism at the Video Music Awards and with her visual album, *Lemonade*.

Meanwhile, Obama designed a racial initiative, My Brother's Keeper, to assist only Black boys in the fight against racism, excluding girls. Misogyny once again was allowed to silently prop up the very racism that supposedly is under attack.

Let us unpack the tensions and conflicts about what it means to be an abolitionist socialist feminist today. The challenge is this: there is no one kind of feminism, although it is often represented as though there were, and that *one* is too often assumed to be white, western-hetero, and liberal or neoliberal.

But feminisms *are* a plurality of one, and that oneness is always multiple, or what I have termed elsewhere, polyversal—many and unified at the same time. Differences and conflict are always ripe with positive potential. Differences should not pose a dilemma for shared commonality. Nuanced shared oppression and power allows for revolutionary alliances.

Women are different and many. Singular identities only give us a single site to connect through. The more ways we are seen by each other, the more possibilities there are for us to connect to each other. If I am seen for the whole of my parts, you will have more entry to know and trust at least parts of me. The work we do together is the beginning of transformation.

As gender has become more differentiated by class, gender is more fractured. As race has become more diversified by class, it needs more specificity. Categories are less homogenous than they once were, and yet they also remain static and punishing. I often feel constrained by the naming of *distinct* categories that are completely interwoven with each other. *I am looking for the points of contact among the overlap that let us see new relationships.* It is here that creative bonds can be formed.

This is why risk and courage are always needed rather than rigid exclusionary categories. Instead of looking to close things off, let us be dangerously curious and look for new places to build solidarities that can help us forge an inclusive politics against misogyny in its entire hetero-militarist, capitalist, able-bodied, racist manifestations.

This is and will remain messy. A connector may be partial and momentary and not last forever. This means coming together when interests are shared and strategic and then building outward from an initial coming together. The tensions and conflicts of such movement building require forthrightness and faithful support and are continuously in process.

Locating sexual violence as a site of important movement work is key to mobilizing in revolutionary feminist ways. Why? Sexual violence cuts through and binds women across class, race, place, and nation. It is ubiquitous and universal and politically salient, even if uniquely individual. And it is too often made politically invisible.

Sexual violence is war in yet another form. Carl von Clausewitz popularized the notion that war is simply politics in another form. To me, rape becomes an invisible site of war through the discourse of sex, which is naturalized. Instead of being political, it becomes invisible, individualized, and naturalized, seemingly inevitable.

So let us make sexual violence/violation politically salient and tell a new truth while doing so. Sexual violence, whether in the workplace, domestic life, gaming, or war, offers a formidable shared location for resistance. It exists alongside other forms of gendered exploitation and affects all women, waged and unwaged, migrant, refugee, and asylum seeker. It is often sidelined by these other oppressions.

Sexual violence in its many and varied complicit forms must be revealed and remedied in any revolutionary feminist imagining. The redress is not retribution or punishment but reconciliation, rehabilitation, and restorative justice. This should radicalize and revolutionize our notions of antiracist, anti-heteropatriarchal feminisms in the struggle for a humane world.

It is troubling that US Secretary of Education Betsy DeVos—one of the many right-wing incompetents to be appointed by Trump—proposed changing and limiting the purview of Title IX and its ability to address sexual violence on college campuses. She argued that legislation had gone too far in protecting sexual *victims* and did not do enough to protect the accused perpetrator. This is part of a regressive attempt to undermine feminism's success at challenging and limiting sexual violence in everyday life. It is a part of the larger right-wing backlash against feminist success, even if it also points to other complex issues of justice that remain to be addressed.

Imagine a revolution that seeks an end to all sexual violence, and that this revolution is as essential as one that respects the climate and the earth and humanity. Women-of-color disproportionately inhabit this world. Much of my thinking about this comes from my work with women of color feminists and the women of One Billion Rising, the global movement founded by Eve Ensler to end rape and sexual violence against women.

Is not the rape of the earth by oil refining, with little regard to the climate and its warming and its extremes, connected to the wanton, hostile mindset toward women's bodies? Would ending this violence disable racist heterosexist capitalist patriarchy? If we end the violence against everything from women's bodies to extractive industries, we flip the planet toward justice and radical abolitionism.

As racial and sexual inequality and environmental plunder have increased to devastate this globe, I have found renewed purpose in connecting the struggle for socialism with antiviolence feminist commitments. This explicitly targets the sexual politics of violence that resides inside racial and economic oppression. It targets the carceral state with its prison system and policing apparatus. As psychologist and former director of mental health for the Massachusetts prison system James Gilligan makes so very clear, our prisons are steeped in sexual violence. Rape occurs routinely and regularly. It is used to perpetuate and institutionalize fear and control.

My theorizing point here: abolitionism must embrace revolutionary antiviolence, antiracist feminisms, with bodily and earth justice for all.

V. WHY SOCIALIST FEMINISM IS NOT ENOUGH

What does Marxist or socialist feminism mean for the present moment? New formulations of states, politics, proletariats, and materialisms are in order. This query derives from my use of historical materialism as a method that I think with and through. I use a Marxist materialism to contextualize and historicize not only economic class, but race and genders and their changed relationship to each other.

Marxists today need to be explicitly abolitionist anti-racist feminists. Marx denormalized, denaturalized, and historicized class relations. I use his method to denaturalize and historicize class and extend it to explain gendered racism and sexualized white supremacy. This expands and enlarges the meaning of materialism beyond production to a historical materialism of racialized heteropatriarchy. I use the skeletal class framework Marx offered to more fully materialize sexual production, sexual reproduction, racialized sexuality, and white supremacy.

For me, capitalism is not a singular system, so neither is class as its core. One cannot add up sex, race, and class as though they were separate. Each is intertwined with the other. Whatever the conditions of economic class, they are connected through a history of racist sexual violence and gendered labor. Out of this recognition emerge possibilities to form and marshal a new camaraderie, a new proletariat that is composed overwhelmingly of women. This understanding of proletariat is global and demands an anti-imperial, antiracist, antiviolence revolution.

Socialist feminism needs to embrace an inclusive understanding of power relations, not deductive and reductive notions of class. I want to further broaden, refocus, and extend the aspects of class exploitation without reducing them to economic/productive formulations. I do not want to incorporate sexuality, race, and gender into class.

Materialize—specify the actual body's physicality. Stop assuming that the body is an essentialist category. Materializing female bodies (trans, nongendered, etc.) means they must be contextualized in terms of their racialized sexual specificity and possible reproductive capacities as well as their specific forms of exploitation and oppression. Capitalism and racist patriarchy and neoliberal misogyny need a full materialist accounting of their mutual dependence and semi-autonomous standing. Neoliberalism is the present ideology justifying excessive capitalism.

Although I was one of the early authors of the term *socialist feminist*, after the 1989 fall of the Soviet Union, the term no longer seemed viable to me. With much critique and contempt toward socialism from women in Russia and the former Yugoslavia and surrounding countries, the use of such an identity seemed unproductive. Added to this was the ignorance and hostility toward socialism in western capitalist countries at the time, making it seem like a futile political position. But as class exploitation increased with a vengeance toward women and girls, especially those in third world south countries, I shifted yet again to the tyranny of exploitation and the need for socialist feminism.

Bernie Sanders has popularized the idea of socialism of late, whatever the public thinks he means by it. This is an opportunity for #Feminism4the99 to extend their politics and the commitments of the Occupy movement to attack the mutual dependence of capitalist racism and sexist capitalism on each other and their relatively autonomous relationshiop to each other.

In the early 1990s I attended meetings of the Network of East-West Women, made up of women from all over the former Soviet Union, parts of Eastern Europe, and the United States. Our purpose was simply to talk with each other and find our commonalities, while also discovering our differences.

Many Russian women thought that US feminists suffered from a naiveté about equality. The Eastern European feminists were highly critical of the way the *so-called* socialist states had appropriated the language of women's equality and sexual equality for the purposes of the state, not women.

Most Eastern European women felt they had been triply oppressed in the name of equality. They worked in the labor force, worked in the home as domestics and mothers, and were the mainstay of consumer labors such as the shopping to maintain the household, which always required too much time given long bread lines and other problems of supply. There were many similarities with Black feminist critiques of US white mainstream feminism.

Although daycare was provided by the state at the time, many of the Eastern European women were not pleased with the care. And overseeing the care and the pickups and drop-offs of children was still the woman's responsibility. The women were tired of *equality* if it meant they were responsible for home and family life after a long day of work. They needed no more of it. So they saw mainstream feminists in the United States like Betty Friedan as naïve and wrongheaded when they encouraged women to join the workforce without any political or economic support.

Russian women, again much like US Black women, were also critical of the notion that abortion rights were coequal with the notion of women's rights. For many, abortion had been forced on them as a mode of contraception. Several of the women I met had had more than ten abortions. Without access to contraception, the right to abortion often felt like a punitive choice to them. They wanted access to contraceptives first, abortions second. They demanded reproductive rights to their bodies, which are more expansive than simply abortion rights.

These East-West dialogues were very instructive to me. I saw that one's cultural and political context have everything to do with the meaning of political words and their impact on feminisms across the globe. At the time of these meetings, Russia had the most open abortion policy of any country in the world. Today, Putin and the Russian rightwing rail against all abortions, along with women's sexual rights.

Fast forward to the Russian feminist rock group Pussy Riot in 2012. They said they would not be cowed by Putin's antiwoman rhetoric and the religious fanaticism of the Russian Orthodox Church. They insisted on performing their music freely wherever they chose, even in one of Moscow's most revered cathedrals. Three of them were arrested the moment they began to perform. Two were jailed and became further politicized in the process.

Pussy Riot's Nadezhda Tolokonnikova wrote an open letter from Penal Colony No. 14 in Mordovia, describing the inhumane conditions she and everyone in the Russian prison system were experiencing, and declaring a hunger strike. She wrote of her life as an inmate, of the fear and intimidation continually used to regulate and discipline and shame prisoners. She wrote that fellow prisoners became the enforcers of the inhumanity. Anyone showing a bit of determination and self-respect was beaten down, both physically and mentally.

She described her prison as a gulag, where inmates were terrorized each hour of each day, of each week, of each month, of each year. This resonates powerfully with critiques by leaders of the US de-carceration movement, led by Black feminists like Ruthie Gilmore and Beth Ritchie. Incarceration in the US penal and detention system is seen as a bedrock of white supremacy, used against Blacks and immigrants. Because it is so bedrock, abolition of the system must be the goal.

Think a bit about Putin. He is very similar to Trump: an open misogynist in his protection of his militarist state. Trump and Putin share a particularly physical and brutish form of patriarchy. They anguish over their manliness, Putin strutting with his bare chest, Trump with his orange comb-over. Their paranoia as white heterosexual rich men determines their antics, which end up exposing the very pillars of state power.

Putin's latest form of nationalism negates and sidelines socialism and communism and western democracy. He uses antifeminist and homophobic discourses to express his particular form of traditional patriarchal nationalism and relies on the Holy Father of the Russian Orthodox Church to help mask state-corporate cronyism. There is hardly a shadow left of the enormous gains made by and for women during the Bolshevik Revolution.

VI. WHY ANTIRACISM IS NEVER ENOUGH

The African American Policy Forum (AAPF) has been central to documenting the facts about what it means to be both Black or of color and also a girl. It makes perfectly clear that racial inequality and suffering is shared by *both* girls and boys of color, even if in somewhat differing forms. And the consequences are equally grave.

AAPF provides data that shows how girls of color are excessively surveilled and punished in school, and in everyday occurrences, especially in comparison to white girls, and then how they are marginalized, ignored, forgotten, and underreported in findings about racism. A more fully nuanced set of policies is very much still needed, one that recognizes that most Black girls are doubly punished, by both exclusion and hypervisibility; that shows that race and gender are *always* simultaneously present; and that singular notions of racism are incomplete.

Yet, and in contrast, there has been a new visibility of Black women with Michelle Obama as first lady, Loretta Lynch as Attorney General, Stephanie Rawlings-Blake in Baltimore as mayor, and Marilyn Mosby as the state's attorney for Baltimore. There is no simple inside/outside as new identities and borders are crossed. The visibility of powerful Black women contrasts deeply with the invisibility of the Black and Brown women who are disproportionately beaten, raped, killed, and incarcerated.

Kim Crenshaw, cofounder of AAPF and originator of the term "intersectionality," has been crucial in articulating the particular relationship between racism and patriarchy for Black women and girls. She was unrelenting in her criticism of Obama's signature racial initiative, My Brother's Keeper, a program creating "outreach and new opportunities" for Black and Latino boys and men only. Girls and women of color have been excluded, ignored, and sidelined as though the problem of racial inequality does not affect them.

Crenshaw indicts this singular approach to the problem of race as seriously disabling for girls of color. She calls it an approach that leaves an exclusionary notion of racism as part of Obama's legacy. Crenshaw proposes redesigning and redirecting efforts away from an either/or lens towards a race-based policy that includes all genders. This critical response towards My Brother's Keeper attempts to make it inclusive rather than exclusionary. It is not positioned against Black boys and men, but takes the racial umbrella and enlarges it to cover the multiple communities of color across gender and sexual lines.

Given her commitment to intersectional feminism, Kim Crenshaw helped to organize a public antiracist feminist response to Obama's initiative. First a group of men of color wrote a public letter in criticism of the exclusion of Black girls and women. Then a group of Black women and women of color added their voices. The letters were circulated for signatures and were well received, but with little response from the White House. Kim next asked a group of white feminists to create a letter expressing their concern about the inadequacy of My Brother's Keeper for women of color and showing their support for the women and men of color who had spoken out against the program's exclusionary stance.

Working on the letter with the group of white feminists reminded me of the time in the early 1970s when Black feminists demanded a critique from white feminists that would address the need for racial as well as gender inclusivity in the movement. They insisted on a needed corrective that recognized racial differences as part of any conversation about gender, because gender comes in every color. And now, as white women, we were being asked to stand with them to say that race comes in more than one gender. As such, My Brother's Keeper needed to be enlarged to include girls and women of color alongside their fathers, brothers, cousins, and friends.

The letter from our group read in part:

. . . to the extent that racial injustice exists in collusion with gender injustice and sexual violence, it is in the interest of all women—whatever the color—to stand together against the privilege that underpins misogyny. As white feminists, we seek full equality for all people of color, boys and girls, men and women, gay and straight and trans alike. In the year 2017, it is time to fully recognize the intersections and overlap of gender and race. Our country is not color blind, or blind to gender. We should not let the signature racial initiative by President Obama be one that excludes gender. Let us put both and all in view. There are few moments that may allow any of us to really make a difference. But this may be one that does. And given the many years that women have learned from each other and struggled together to mix and blend our commitments across racial, sexual, gender, and class lines, it is time for us to take public action as such. Let us focus here, rather than on the fractures that make it difficult to see this possibility of community in this moment.

We planned to ask white women to sign the letter if they agreed that the inequalities of race and gender exist threaded together. In this world that is imploding with too many singular sectarian campaigns, this was a moment to stand against exclusionary identities. We hoped that there would be a massive response and then maybe a fabulous outcome.

We finished the writing over several months and were ready to launch the letter for signatures when the police murdered Michael Brown. It became an impossible moment to circulate a letter written by white women on behalf of Black women and girls against their exclusion. Black feminists are too often written off by many in Black communities as being race traitors to Black men. Our white feminist voices on behalf of Black women in the aftermath of the brutal killing of Michael Brown would not assist our Black sisters nor the coalitional abolitionist feminist work we were wanting.

Out of this crisis, however, grew a different effort to expose the racist misogynist web of power. Kimberlé and AAPF launched the #SayHerName campaign to draw attention to all the Black women who were also being killed by police. A vigil was held in New York City to recognize the unjust deaths of these many Black women. We gathered with their mothers to simply say these women's names.

Rekia Boyd, Natasha McKenna, Yvette Smith, Miriam Carey, Shelly Frey, Darnisha Harris, and Tanisha Anderson are some of the black women who have died at the hands of police right alongside Trayvon Martin, Michael Brown, Tamir Rice, Philando Castile, and too many others. Yet there are no marches in their name. There has been too little media coverage or anger and outcry. Instead there has been deafening silence about these deaths, despite the fact that 20 percent of unarmed Blacks killed in the last fifteen years by police were women.

Black women's lives matter too. As the Combahee River Collective wrote in 1977 in response to the serial killings and rapes of Black women in Boston, those women died because they were both female and Black. Sexual violence and rape are the more usual forms of racist treatment of Black and Brown women, and their race and gender make them twice vulnerable.

The Combahee River Collective authored one of the first and most lasting manifestoes on Black feminism, which recognized the multiple and overlapping oppressions defining Black women, lesbian and straight. The statement on Black feminism was first published in its entirety in 1979 in my book, *Capitalist Patriarchy and the Case for Socialist Feminism*. This historic statement declared that racism, sexism, heterosexism, and capitalism are interlocking systems of oppression that necessitate revolutionary actions. The collective's contribution had a rebirth and celebration at the National Women's Studies Association Meeting in 2017.

The story of Black women's invisibility alongside the violence perpetrated against her continues. Marissa Alexander was jailed in 2010 for defending herself against an abusive husband, as are countless other women in domestic abuse situations. After finally being released from prison, Marissa has become an advocate for imprisoned women and their children, fighting for decarceration. The injustice in Marissa's case is stark. At the same time she was found guilty, George Zimmerman, who shot and killed Trayvon Martin, was found innocent of murder.

Trayvon died at Zimmerman's hand, while no one was killed when Marissa tried to defend herself and her children with a gun. Marissa tried to use the same Stand Your Ground law as Zimmerman did, but to no avail. She had an eight-day-old baby at the time of her incarceration. Other outrages are legion: serial rapist Daniel Holtzclaw, for example, a police officer, raped multiple Black women in his custody before any action was taken to stop him.

Angela Davis describes chattel slavery as a system of brutalization and oppression that remains present today in the prison-industrial complex. This is especially true for women of color, she says. In the case of Black women, patriarchy may liken them to white women in some instances, seeing them as less "dangerous" than Black men, but the filters of white supremacy create contradictory meanings.

Black women are the fastest growing segment of the US prison population. Black and LatinX women are suspended from school at a higher rate than white women. They are murdered and unemployed at higher rates. Without dealing with racism, misogyny remains in place, and without attacking misogyny, racism marches on. Police violence, sexual violence, and domestic violence are webbed with each other, as are racism and misogyny and heterosexism in their different class configurations.

By now Sandra Bland's name is well known. If she had had bail money, she would still be alive. A twenty-eight-year-old Black woman is stopped by a white police officer. She sees the police officer in her rearview mirror and tries to get out of his way. He pulls her over for moving lanes without using her signal. She gets a ticket, which is a bit of an overreach in and of itself.

She is annoyed and bothered; who would not be? But the officer gets more annoyed and nasty and loses his temper. It seems irrational, given the origin of the stop. He tells her to put out her cigarette. She refuses. She is told to get out of the car, probably illegally, and then is manhandled, and pulled out of her car, and thrown to the ground. She is arrested for this minor traffic violation.

What started out as an ordinary day, July 10, 2015, turned tragic for Sandra, Sandy to her friends. Instead of receiving a ticket and going on her way, she was terrorized by a policeman, arrested, thrown in jail, and had bail set at five thousand dollars. The bail was outrageous and excessive. She had no history with the law and yet was made to stay in jail until the bond could be paid. Bail became a punishment without any due process, ending in her tragic death.

She was isolated in a cell by herself for three days. And then she was found hanged in her cell. Instead of total outrage at this, the news media questioned her actions. Was she unruly, was she using drugs, was she depressed? And ultimately, did she commit suicide? Sandra Bland had no culpability here. None. Instead, the arresting officer and judge who set the bail were and are to blame.

Sandra Bland was condemned to death as a Black woman, having nothing to do with who she was as an individual. This is what a white supremacist patriarchal justice system looks like. You have no rights or effective legal protections to defend yourself in moments like these. And if you do not have money for bail, you may die.

In a sane world, everyone—especially white people—would be asking how this could happen. They would be outraged that Bland was arrested in the first place, that a punishing bail was set, that she had to suffer even an hour locked up. Instead, there are queries about her worthiness as an individual.

The problem here is not Sandra Bland or any of the other recent victims of police violence and carceral state abuse. Since her death, several more women of color have been found dead in their jail cells. Sandra Bland was innocent of any actionable wrongdoing on the day she was incarcerated. She did not deserve to die. Sandra Bland had no more rights on July 10, 2015, than she would have had as an enslaved Black woman in chattel slavery. No laws protected her, just as they would not have protected her in slavery. However she died, she was murdered by an unforgiving system of white supremacist capitalist patriarchy. She died because of an overly punishing and retrograde police state. Police and policing have become violent beyond sanity. This is what neoslavery looks like in the twenty-first century.

Before the funeral, Sandra's mother, Geneva Reed-Veal, a single mother of five girls, said she would bury her daughter and then turn to seeking justice. "Once I put this baby in the ground, I'm ready. This means war."

On the three-year anniversary of Sandra Bland's death, historians Keisha Blain and Phillip Sinitiere hosted a public forum on the African American Intellectual Historical Society website. Writers discussed police violence, white supremacist patriarchy, the surveillance state, African American history in the US South, #BlackLivesMatter, Black feminism, #SayHerName, and the carceral state.

VII. THE WHITE MIND AND ITS INJUSTICES

I listened to Juror B29 apologize to Trayvon Martin's mother and I could not quite fathom it. The juror said she was hurting and was deeply devastated by her part in the acquittal. She said that Zimmerman was guilty of murder and got away with it. But why did he?

I think that the almost all-white, all-female jury did not try to imagine themselves as Trayvon on that night, or as though he were their son. Instead they appeared to identify more with Zimmerman and his alleged fearfulness. They saw the so-called facts through a prism of white (female) racial privilege, right along with the judge's reading of the law. They, including Juror B29—though Puerto Rican—could not assign "intent" to Zimmerman.

White privilege, and its protection in a veil of neutrality, is the racial problem in this case. Race applies to whiteness. Yet white people are not "raced" per se because they are the standard. A person of color is most often described as such, whereas a white person is not. Hillary Clinton was described as a female candidate, not as a white one. Barack Obama was described as a Black candidate.

This leads to the problem of the "white mind," which is not a biological category, but rather a way of seeing. This mindset privileges what is seen and interpreted through a lens that defers to a false rationality, to an assumed abstract inclusiveness known as individualism, to the scientific model of supposed cause and effect, and to the artificial dichotomous viewing of either/or. Complexity and multiplicity are pushed away. Law, especially criminal law, is deeply embedded in this white-mind framework.

Whiteness is a method of knowing, hearing, and thinking. It clings to a notion of universality, objectivity, and neutrality instead of specificity, historicity, subjectivities, and disparate outcomes. Truths and falsities with no grey areas dominate. People are indoctrinated in the notion of *abstract* individualism as though it is extended to all, rather than to a few—by race, class, sex, gender, and ableism. The more abstract and ahistorical the stance, the more easily the years of chattel slavery are forgotten and white privilege is normalized.

I am all for the careful, reasonable, and rational use of law. But this is not the same as a rationalized, normalized whiteness, or rationalized, naturalized heterosexist misogyny. When bifurcation of thought undermines the possibility of complexity and diversity of meanings in the name of rationality, it licenses murder. The white legal mind, as such, is deadly.

Supposedly, the law—post-slavery and Jim Crow—is color-blind, but little else in life is, so both the interpretation and the application of law are race- and sex-biased and subjective, no matter what the law intends. Given this limitation, *the law can at best be used to create justice by controlling for racial bias, and by recognizing that race matters. As such, the law should never be assumed to be just.*

To say that the law itself requires an acquittal in a particular case continues to abstract and legitimize law. But even supposedly fair laws are always already contaminated. The law is never completely objective or unbiased. It cannot be. US law was written by white propertied men with other white propertied men in mind. There is no mention or recognition that law is raced at its heart. Nor that it is gendered or sexed or class-based.

Chief Justice Rehnquist often referred to the Constitution as not mentioning pregnant persons, or women, nor meaning to include them—whether discussing veterans' rights or abortion. The only way to counter this bias is to see and think and decipher with the heart of a female person of color. This viewing is not subjective in and of itself. It is rather a corrective for the racist bias of the law. It is critical that the Trayvon Martin case was said to *not* be about race or racial profiling by the prosecutors and white female judge.

I think that race is not simply coded by one's skin color, although it most often is. This is why mixed-race juries are needed even if they are not always the deal breaker one hopes for. The whiteness of the (in)justice system is complexly structured through implicit bias and prejudice.

Given this, an all-white jury is always problematic. But Juror B29 does not speak to this issue easily. Maybe through intimidation by the otherwise white jury, she voted like a white woman, despite her color. Or maybe, instead of seeing the problem of race in the legal narrative, she looked to the law to resolve racism, which it cannot do.

Where and when does white privilege begin? This white-mind bias was true again in the murder of Michael Brown. Hearts broke once more in communities of color across this country. Black Lives Matter activists mobilized in Ferguson, Missouri, to say no to the militarized policing and unrelenting surveillance and murder of Black bodies.

Historically, lynching and castration were readily used against Black males. Given white women's accusatory role in early rape narratives, white supremacy and sexual violence has a deep problematic history. White womanhood plays a troublesome part here that complicates Black women's response to the violence. Yet today, Black women and girls, especially trans women, are targeted and raped and violated by brutal racism. The tactics are not identical, but yet shared. Racism does not extend gender privilege to Black women, even if it may appear to do so.

White feminists need to stand with our sisters of color against the brutalization of Black male bodies while also standing with them against their invisibility in the fight against heteromisogyny. To keep Black women invisible is to assist the patriarchal and misogynist support systems of racism. White masculinity, militarism, and misogyny prop up racism, which punishes all Blacks across sex and gender and class.

Patriarchy may liken Black women to white women in some ways, but it never gives them the same privilege. And the criminalization and dehumanization of Black people does not spare or protect Black women. Racism should not be used to silence or ignore the sexism that is *in/and of* racism itself. To do so makes Black women invisible.

VIII. AND THEN THERE WAS THE 2016 ELECTION

Many women had their qualms about Hillary Clinton: too elitist, too beholden to corporate interests, too implicated in Bill Clinton's racially constructed carceral state. Despite these misgivings, given the immensely misogynist and racist campaign of Donald Trump, Black and LatinX women voted overwhelmingly for Hillary Clinton. They did not need to be in total harmony with Hillary in order to vote against Trump's misogynoir.

On the other hand, white women across all class lines voted in greater numbers for Trump, with fifty-three percent supporting him. (Whites as a whole preferred Trump over Clinton by some 20 percentage points: 58 percent for him, 37 percent for her.) But remember that almost half of the eligible voters did not vote at all. And that Hillary eventually amassed three million more votes than Trump.

It is still unfathomable to me that anyone who demonizes people of color, immigrants, and Muslims and is so ignorant and hateful to these communities could be a viable candidate, let alone president. This makes me wonder whether his misogynist bravado actually legitimated his assault as a partial cover and diversion for his racism, that his racism and Islamophobia were mobilized and authorized by his misogynist posturing. And wonder is all I can do: how exactly his complex set of prejudices and hatreds and fears stoke his policies.

Did many white women vote against Hillary Clinton because they absorbed and supported the misogynist rhetoric used against her? As such they did not trust her. Maybe these white women felt reassured by Trump's masculinist rhetoric of the good old white supremacist days. Possibly a white supremacist patriarchy they already knew felt less threatening than a multiracial world that they did not.

Were white women willing to vote for the guy promising to make them "great again," keeping their white privilege intact, even if it meant leaving patriarchal misogyny in place? Once again, I suspect that the fact that whites will be a minority very soon in the United States frightens racist white women. As the United States becomes less white (and also more gender fluid), does the racial hierarchy of white womanhood lose its potency and protectiveness?

Why did white women fail to do what Black and LatinX women did: vote against the racist misogynist-in-chief? There is nothing new about recognizing that women do not/cannot vote as a bloc. But what is it about white women that explains why they voted for a racist misogynist? It would not be the first time that white women supported patriarchy in order to protect white privilege.

Historically, many white women supported rape and lynching narratives that demonized Black men while protecting white male rapists, often their own husbands. Lynchings supposedly protected white womanhood, while Black women suffered the sexual violence of white men. In her book, *Southern Horrors*, Crystal Feimster shows how patriarchy may subjugate white women as it seemingly protects them and privileges them as "white." The pedestal has always been problematic, but many white women have not been willing to give it up.

I thought that the 2016 election would prove this alliance between white women and men wrong: that white women would vote alongside women of color against (racist) misogyny. Instead, their ease with misogynoir seeped inside the voting booth. I think that these white women feel more comfortable navigating misogyny— Trump seems like many of the men they already know and manage—and a world without white supremacy feels too frightening and unknown.

Tragically, too many white women betrayed the possibility of cross-racial solidarity. Although most white mainstream feminists voted for Clinton, other (white) women did not. I thought the incredible struggle by women of color for the past three decades to confront the privileging of whiteness had brought about change and done more to uproot white privilege than it has.

Yet I do not want to give up the commitment of a multiracial, multiclass women's movement and larger revolutionary possibilities just because of the wreckage that both Trump's election and Clinton's campaign has left us with. Clinton's neoliberal feminist agenda was insufficient for way too many women and others. Yet women of color rallied in spite of this. The rubble created by the white women's vote is for antiracist white women to address.

I remain committed to building connectors between women of color and antiracist white women in the continued struggle against economic, racial, and gender inequality. I do not want to live in a world that cannot commit to this. But the struggle demands complete focus on the part of antiracist white feminists to build cross-class alliances against racist misogyny. This struggle will transform us and the working class simultaneously. This election of Trump is on us, even more than it is on Hillary Clinton.

IX. WHEN THE CRITIQUE OF CAPITAL(ISM) IS NOT ENOUGH

Why does Thomas Piketty write a book titled *Capital* and ignore the underpinnings of wealth as an accumulation of profit from racism and patriarchy? Even more important, why is his work so applauded by progressives and mainstream economists as a landmark book when he views capital as though it operates singularly? Maybe this should be no surprise at all. But to affirm his blindspots is to carry them forth.

He claims that population growth deeply influences wealth and therefore capital, but there is no recognition of the sexual reproductive labor that is the source of population growth. He shows that global population growth peaked during the years between 1950 and 1970. These were key years of women's domesticity—enormous hours of stolen, free domestic labor *for* capital by all women, most especially by women of color.

Piketty focuses especially on eighteenth-century Europe and the United States. The eighteenth century is defined by the slave trade and yet there is no analysis of how capital accumulation and slave labor, or slave rape, grossly sustained each other. He recognizes that enslaved peoples were used as property and added to capital, but there is no recognition of the sexual reproduction of labor by Black enslaved women, exacerbated by rape, as part of market value or capital.

Inequality in the twenty-first century cannot be redressed without addressing its racist history of chattel slavery. Piketty recognizes that brutal racial inequality persists today but believes it has no specific standing in relation to capital. Sexual trafficking that both reflects the brutality of economic inequality and contributes with stolen labor to the very structuring of global capital remains unrecognized and undertheorized.

Piketty says "capital is not an immutable concept"; it reflects prevailing social relations. This is why *both* patriarchy and racism should be key to his understanding. Labor—the other side of capital—comes in colors and races and sexes and genders and is formulated through new expressions of power. Racialized and sexualized and gendered labor contributes to capital accumulation and structures the inequality emanating from it.

Excessive economic inequality is always further intensified by racial and gender configurations. The inequality

ABOLITIONIST SOCIALIST FEMINISM

is not simply excessive; it is particularly excessive according to race and sex. White and heteropatriarchal privilege form a regenerative structuring of power for capital. Rich and poor nations modernize within these inequitable constraints.

It is past time for a more inclusive understanding of the economy, of capital, of profit, of inequality. Without this there cannot be justice for humanity in its entirety. The world is witnessing the chaos of capital(ism) given the excesses of the one percent. The Occupy movement put the unfairness of the system in view. It is now past due to connect the overlapping systems of global capitalism, gross inequality, and sexual, gendered, and racial oppression. Without this recognition, each is left to support the other.

There are many new forms of women's labor that assist capital: service, technological, domestic, transnational caregiving, and so forth. Patriarchal exploitation targets women and girls as the newest migrants of the globe. Meanwhile, sexual violence travels from private and familial sites to varied public work places as documented in the #MeToo movement. Too often, the sexual violence underwrites the waged exchange.

In 2014, the largest fast food strike in the history of the world took place. It extended from New York City to New Zealand to Brazil. The workers demanded a living wage of fifteen dollars an hour in the United States. Disproportionate numbers of the demonstrators were women of color. These women make up the current proletariat of this globe and are the biggest resource for capital. They orchestrated the strike against a two-hundred-billion-dollar industry, calling attention to excessive greed, especially of the CEOs.

Despicable working conditions for millions are the other side of the excessive wealth of a few. This injustice was put on view for all to see when the Rana Plaza building in Savar, Bangladesh, collapsed to the ground, trapping thousands of garment workers, mostly women. Approximately 1,100 of them died, and another 1,400 suffered grave injury. Men also suffer from devastating working conditions. In Soma, Turkey, coal miners often die on the job. Great wealth alongside grinding poverty colludes with a horrific misogynist racism to define today's global workforce.

Visible and invisible labor, derivative of the sexual division of labor, are part of capital production. Labor, profit, and capital each contain extraction from a complex whole that includes the myriad ways in which women's unpaid work supports the system. Viewing inequality in a singular way protects it. Since women's and girl's toiling bodies are integral to capital and its attendant inequality, they must therefore be integral to abolitionist socialist feminism too.

Piketty ends his book by saying that we must risk

everything and think more creatively in order to get hold of the runaway capitalist train. But he does not risk enough. So let us risk more and and call for an abolitionist socialist feminist revolution. Meanwhile, I will agree with him that we can at least start by *really* taxing the rich.

X. WHEN THE POPE'S PONTIFICATIONS ARE NOT ENOUGH

Blindness to racist misogyny repeats itself with Pope Francis. He criticizes unbridled capitalism for its injustice. He has been applauded widely and loudly for this and should be. But a critique of the complicity of unbridled patriarchy and racist misogyny is also needed, from both him and his many supporters. A condemnation of, and the resolve to end, sexual violation and rape by huge numbers of priests is long overdue as well.

It is common knowledge that the majority of the poor across the globe and 70 percent of the world's refugees are women and children, disproportionately of color. It is therefore not possible to redress worldwide inequality and poverty without dealing with the patriarchal racist sexual division of labor, along with the related sexual trafficking and sexual violence toward women. The United Nations reports that one in three women and girls have experienced physical or sexual violence in their lifetime. This amounts to one billion people. Yet Pope Francis stays far from these realities. Women of all colors remain hidden in plain sight.

The newest fashions of excessive capitalism have their own new unfettered racist patriarchy. The tyranny is male-centric and heterosexist. It breeds a culture of exclusion that Pope Francis silently endorses. And sometimes, as in his 2014 "State of the World Address," he explicitly denies women the right to control their own bodies by condemning abortion as "horrific" and part of our "throw away" society.

Without the right to choose contraception and abortion there is no justice for women. The sexual rights of women—rights to their bodies—must be claimed. There is also no justice without the full inclusion of gays and the related freedoms of sexual and gender choice. And without fully exposing the secrets and supposed shame of sexual violation—pedophilia and rape—there can be no meaningful justice for anyone.

All that is significant about Pope Francis's challenge to the rightward drift and its domination of the Catholic Church is dimmed by his continued avoidance of the patriarchal suffering of women and girls. This suffering is quietly left in place and also in plain sight. This is true for all who have been sexually violated, both within and outside the Church. And it pertains to contraception. A world with no contraception would be a world of even greater poverty. Pope Francis simply assumes that women will use birth control and keep the open secret to themselves.

In his 2013 apostolic exhortation, *Evangelii Gaudium*, Pope Francis condemns the evils of hunger, violence, and the "idolatry of money" without connecting them to the objectification of people's bodies, male and female, in all their gender-variant forms. He is horrified by the years-long wars fought over mineral extraction in the Congo and simply avoids the fact that it has been grotesquely fought on the bodies of women through rape. Sexual violence is entangled in the Congo's investment in its mining sector. And it tumbles outwards toward everyone in its path, young boys and girls included.

Pope Francis says that the "structural causes" of poverty must be eliminated, but capitalism remains the only structure he addresses. Our violent and starving globe is as patriarchal and racialized as it is capitalist. Socialist feminists and radical feminists have been making this argument for decades. The Nuns on the Bus, a group of radical nuns who tour the United States with their critique of wealth, have embraced and popularized the idea that the Church should be for the 99 percent. It is significant that no nun has been suspended for lavish spending, as some male bishops have, yet women are not thought worthy of ordination.

Much of the violence of poverty is racist and patriarchal in form. New locations of sexual violence develop with new structural relations of labor. Women in the Philippines constitute a particularly large portion of domestic workers throughout the world. How is it they do not deserve inclusion in a notion of justice that would afford them bodily autonomous rights?

As more women of color have become migrant workers, leaving their home countries to do caregiving work elsewhere, they become transnational laborers, living far from their families. They provide domestic labor and childcare for wealthier, very often white, families, while their own families suffer. This aggressive form of capitalist racist patriarchy has shifted half of all migrant labor toward women, who are vulnerable to sexual abuse since they work with few protections. Women put themselves in harm's way with little choice. The new, global, transnational households that women are forced to create because of the excessive greed of global capitalist racist heteropatriarchy should, by their existence, discredit the Pope's bifurcation of the economy, which splits off women's labor from their lives and their bodies.

Justice must include all female bodies and their needs, both for freedom from sexual abuse and economic want and for freedom to choose whatever they might need: contraception, abortion, or a full-term pregnancy. The severing of women *from* the economy and *from* their bodies is the real injustice and violence. Controlling one's reproductive life is part of determining one's economic productive life. Poverty is intimately connected to the ability to choose what female bodies will and will not do.

Pope Francis perpetuates the notion that the political economy is not sexed and raced, that personal life is not intimately connected to the public market. He bifurcates, privatizes, and depoliticizes women's bodies, inadvertently maintaining the Church's secrets. And the larger narratives surrounding him and his critique of capitalism, secular and not, further deify this unjust rendering of the present crisis.

Injustice for Pope Francis is about economic suffering. But we—men and women, nonbinary, gender variant, gays and trans, people of all colors—suffer from the particular way other *structural* identities intersect with, and in, the economy. Suffering is more than economic and will remain grossly unequal as long as it is dealt with in this partial fashion. The male-centric heterosexist views of the Church may be disguised in anticapitalist rhetoric, but they remain intact. This is utterly revealed in the repeated exposure of molesting and predator priests.

I was uneasy as the US Supreme Court reviewed the right of corporations to their religious beliefs in order to allow them to refuse to pay for contraceptives for women employees. It is deeply troubling that the Church and state operate to form a kind of "sexularism" once again that denies women's rights in favor of a religiosity that has burst the boundaries of the secular state.

In a homily delivered in May 2018, Pope Francis compared all women to Mary and wrote of unleashing the spiritual energy of women as mothers to improve the world. He stated that women should be given more authority and access to decision making in the Church, but should not be ordained. This will not do. Nor will his stance on abortion. He reiterates the Church's position that a fetus is a person with full rights to protection, with no interest in repositioning a woman's rights in any way. He has no new curiosity or thoughtfulness about women's lives and the reasons for their poverty today.

Pope Francis nobly chooses to personally decline excess and wealth. He happily lives more simply than previous pontiffs. But he does not sufficiently critique the institutional wealth of the Vatican, nor does he suggest a redistribution of its enormous wealth to its masses. Personal and political, individual and structural power are not one and the same.

The biggest travesty that Pope Francis continuously perpetrates is his misogynist racism and heterosexist noninclusive notion of "justice" right alongside the critique of capitalism. He continues the whispers and silences about sexual violence and sexual and gender rights to contraception and abortion. And he remains complicit in the sexual harm done to thousands of his congregants.

The true problem here is hardly Pope Francis alone, but all who continue this discourse as though critiquing the violence of capitalism without condemning patriarchy, sexual violation, and capitalism's racist underpinnings is sufficient for creating justice for us *all*.

XI. THE PROLETARIAT IS NOT WHITE MEN

The world seems upside down. The one percent turns most of our lives towards their benefit. Truth tellers go to jail and liars go free; security trumps democracy; Julian Assange purports to demand transparency from governments while progressives simply forget that he is charged with rape; right-wing activists attack a woman's rights to her body, especially to abortion, while denying real opportunities and the basic necessities to children everywhere; and more people of color than ever are becoming refugees and homeless.

So much is changing: the earth and the weather, and with them, jobs, classes, races, genders, and sexes. Feminisms must change also, because women's lives are changing everywhere. And since so much does not change and stagnates for women and girls, the remaining structural aspects of misogyny still need to be redressed.

Enter the new proletariats—women the world over for whom class still matters, but in new, dispersed and complex ways. Maybe it is time to retrieve the term *proletariat* from Marx and reinvent it for abolitionist socialist feminists. I write "maybe" because I am not sure it matters what we name this massive diverse grouping of some three billion women in all their colors. So much of the depiction of the working class is a distortion. The global working class has never been predominantly white. And many white workers of this working class are not Trump supporters: they hate their bosses more than they love Trump. So, as I wonder whether to think of women as constituting a new working class, I wish to not reproduce misrepresentations of old.

However, I am sure that it is time to recognize the struggle to control women's bodies in all forms—from sexual abuse and rape to the war on abortion to the denial of equal pay—as deeply, politically misogynist even if there is no easy way to mobilize collectively against this effort.

This proletariat of women is named by and for the structural location that women inhabit in the system of labor exchange and its enforcement by sexual abuse and punishment. Girls and women do labor of every sort—domestic, peasant farming, migrant, agricultural, reproductive, consumer, affective, slave, and many other types of waged labor. Birthing, which is actually called labor, is done exclusively by women. Much of this new proletariat includes sex workers in all their variety, as well as the migrant female laborers crisscrossing the globe, the women and girls hauling water and gathering wood, and the *dagongmei* in China, transient women workers who toil in mind-numbing factories for companies like Apple.

It is no small point that so many of the women and girls in the Congo and Rwanda who have been brutally raped and murdered were out laboring—gathering firewood. These proletarian women constitute a sex class of sorts, as a *silenced secret*. Gender continues to morph. This means that what women do and are expected to do is in continual flux. Hillary Clinton spoke of breaking the glass ceiling. I am concerned with getting most of us out of the basement.

Four in ten mothers in the United States are primary breadwinners and upwards of 80 percent of women contribute significantly to the economic well-being of their households. Yet too many women remain poor despite all their hard work, and their race and nation still play a huge role in this.

The disparate realities of women's lives today are more evident than ever. As economic inequality grows, so does the difference between white women and women of other colors. This intensifies as progress is made for a few, while the majority remains in well-established ghettoes.

It would be a mistake to ignore the progress for some,

most often white, women, but also problematic to not recognize that for many women of color there is not enough relief. In the United States, the median net wealth of Black American households is expected to fall to zero by 2053. This means that half of all Blacks will have no net worth by then.

The US military ended the draft and became a voluntary army in 1973, the same year that *Roe v. Wade* was decided, making abortion a legal right for women. The affirmation that women have a constitutional right to choose abortion stands alongside the denial of women's actual sexual rights to their bodies in the military, where sexual harassment and rape continue to be a critical problem. And now, in 2019, legalized abortion hangs by a thread given Trump's choice of Neil Gorsuch and Brett Kavanaugh for the Supreme Court.

The story of women's labor and related struggles continues across the globe. I was recently in Vietnam, and in the mountains outside Sapa, Vietnamese women were everywhere, doing every kind of work. They were relentless in laboring for their families. They are the backbone and energy of their communities. In meetings with them, I also learned how they suffer from domestic violence and rape. I thought back to the Vietnam War and its particular trauma for Vietnamese women and my participation in the 1971 Women's March against the Pentagon, and my antiwar activism.

The Arab Spring brought new promises for women in Tunisia and Egypt, but too soon men were patrolling the streets, punishing women for their activism. Women in Afghanistan have been demanding their education and are brave and tireless, but still Afghan military forces rape them wantonly. Islamic feminists of all varieties push to democratize sharia law and challenge patriarchy despite violent pushback. In Turkey, Recep Tayyip Erdogan was reelected, allowing him to seize dictatorial rights. When first elected, he decreed that every Turkish woman should have three children and that abortion should be totally illegal.

Brazil had a stint with a female president, Dilma Rousseff, and a female police commander, both promoting women's rights, yet rapes increased, especially of poor women. And the avowed misogynist Jair Bolsonaro was elected by a right-wing mobilization in 2018. Similar problems exist in India. The agonizing rape and death of Jyoti Singh Pandey, who was attacked by the men on a bus she had boarded, mobilized massive antirape demonstrations and revisions of rape law throughout India and across the globe. One Billion Rising took this energy and activated antirape demonstrations in more than 270 countries to challenge this sexual trauma.

There is activism in Guatemala and Mexico against the hundreds of murders of women. Homeless shelters are being created in Haiti, Philippines, and Mogadishu, Somalia. Sexual violence connects women to their laboring bodies and the body of the globe. And women's labor—of birthing, rearing, cooking, and maintaining life, alongside paid work—also connects them to each other. Women who occupy seats of power too often obfuscate these relations of exploitation and oppression.

There are more women in the US labor force than ever before. However, this says little about equality, nor is it indicative of a rearrangement of power. It says more about the recession of 2008 and the disproportionate loss of jobs that men, especially white working-class men, had held. These changes are less about feminisms and women's rights and more about the demands of global racist patriarchal capitalism. Yet women have very often used these changes to empower themselves as individuals.

Women have become the largest part of the new global proletariat despite misogynist racism. Chinese women in auto factories demand higher wages and the right to form unions. Immigrant women from the Philippines and the Caribbean are creating a union for women working as nannies in New York. These women across the globe are the backbone of this struggling proletariat.

Modernized misogyny is no less misogynist than previous versions. The privileging of masculinity exists today but in much more economically diverse and diversified expressions. Chattel slavery once relegated all Blacks to deep poverty, even if there were distinctions of privilege from the manor to the field. Being Black and/or a woman today offers more economic diversity than in the past. The once traditional white heterosexual family of bread-winner male and housekeeper female has given way to much more various forms, such as single-parent families, blended ones, gay, mixed race, trans, and so forth. The malleability of family structures has been phenomenal, but it also maintains established power systems.

Women in Eastern Europe before the fall of the Soviet Union in 1989 already carried the burdens of triple duty of domestic, waged, and consumer labor. Women in many African nations have carried more than their share of life's burdens due to poverty. And women filled the munitions factories during the Second World War in the United States and England.

Poor women in India, Thailand, and Cambodia become surrogate mothers, part of the global outsourcing of pregnancy by wealthy families, with women of other classes contributing to their exploitation. An Iranian woman, Sakineh Mohammadie Ashtiani, was threatened with stoning to death for adultery at the same time that Hillary Clinton was negotiating nuclear agreements with Iran's president. South African president Jacob Zuma boasted of his sexual promiscuity, while women in his country suffered rape and AIDS in devastating numbers.

New feminisms, especially abolitionist socialist ones, must stand together with the new proletariats against the transnational exploitation and violence toward women and girls. The health of women and the planet depends on it.

XII. THE CHAOS OF TRUMP'S WHITE-SUPREMACIST MISOGYNY

Ta-Nehisi Coates says that Trump is our first white president. He means that Trump is the first president who actively utilizes and mobilizes a racist discourse hostile to immigrants, Muslims, and Blacks and other people of color. After all, every president other than Obama was white, and several US presidents owned slaves. The newness of this white supremacy is both very old and yet newly aggressive.

Rather than fully acknowledging Trump's misogyny, Coates says that Trump's white supremacy has a "sexual tint." Coates recognizes the history of slave rape and Trump's braggadocio about sexual assault, but once again, there is no theorizing on the structural status of patriarchal gender. As an alternative, I would argue that Trump is our first white supremacist misogynist president.

His openly misogynist bluster toward women is as significant as his white supremacist swagger. Each envelopes the other in inseparable and synergistic fashion. His sexual predation defines his racist and capitalist policies. His sexism and racism guides and articulates his lies, his missteps, and his abuse. The important question here is not whether Trump is or is not a racist or a sexist—he is both—but how he is an ideologue using ideology to suit his mercurial whims and his harmful agenda.

The old political adage is that politicians cannot afford to become too attached to any particular ideology because they must remain flexible in order to respond to whatever the state demands of them. Nixon was famous for his anticommunist cold-war rhetoric and then unexpectedly opened trade for Coca-Cola with the Soviet Union. His switch was summed up as cold cash replaces the Cold War. Trump seems even more contradictory and relentless.

It also is true that the United States is living near the end of its particular phase as a majoritarian white supremacy nation, and anger, hysteria, and violent backlash have been the response of white supremacists. It just may be that the traditional form of the white supremacist nation state is no longer as functional for global capital as it once was. The United States might be living with the leftovers of an earlier white majority nation that now stands in the way of a more rapacious racial global capitalism and its neoliberal predation.

But the US state—via Trump and the Republicans—may be articulating a new white minority supremacist state. As capitalism and the white supremacists battle, the rest of us are treated to open conflict. Trump is either a last hurrah or the attempt at a new beginning of sorts. Either way, his old-fashioned, white male supremacist grab-them-by-the-crotch approach appears to be mobilizing a resistance against him. Trump exposes a crass macho physicality that may unveil rather than stabilize the very system of power he seeks to protect.

Following this line of thought, it is significant that Trump dropped the largest conventional bomb in the seventeen-year-long war in Afghanistan. He acts boorish and brutish with no articulated foreign policy in place. Trump speaks at the United Nations and threatens North Korea with its total destruction if it continues its belligerent foreign policy. Then he sallies forth to ingratiate himself with Kim Jong-un and promises denuclearization. Trump is a dangerous bully with a massive military arsenal subject to his whim and caprice. He undermines the nuclear nonproliferation agreement with Iran, while simultaneously wooing dictators like Erdogan in Turkey and Sisi in Egypt.

Trump, according to foreign policy expert Phyllis

Bennis, continues US foreign imperial policy but with a particular pattern of brute and illegal force. I wonder if this "raw power" might simply reveal his white male misogynist hysteria. From grabbing pussy to rape to dropping bombs

Trump is a noxious predator who uses a brutish sexual physicality. His cabinet is mostly men. His committee to develop a so-called healthcare bill consisted of thirteen white men. His daughter, Ivanka, says he loves women, and sees no irony when he grabs her thigh or ass. Trump surrounds himself with men like himself. Initially, Steve Bannon and Jeff Sessions mobilized a gladiator-like and mean-spirited white supremacy. There was something particularly misogynistic about their irrational and illegal use of power.

Meanwhile, overly militarized police officers use deadly force against Black bodies, several of them children, perhaps another manifestation of the last gasps of white supremacy hurtling into oblivion. At the same time, Trump has remobilized an antiabortion agenda and an antiwoman health bill that is anticontraception, anti-Planned Parenthood, and transphobic.

His anti-abortion stance is not one issue; it is many. Women of every color and every class are impacted by the need for access to abortion and reproductive rights, but most especially, poor and undocumented women. So abortion is an economic issue. It is a racial issue. And it is a woman's issue. Abortion remains the canary in the mine in that it is always used to test the waters for women's rights.

Still and often, abortion and misogyny are sidelined and misunderstood, even by people who claim to support reproductive rights. Although reproductive rights are raced and economic and poverty is raced and sexed, few public figures grasp this fact. Bernie Sanders decided to support Heath Mello, a mayoral candidate in Omaha, Nebraska, even though Mello has a problematic history on abortion. Sanders's position was that we cannot exclude people who disagree with us on one issue. Sorry, Bernie, abortion is not one issue, and it is not just any issue. Nancy Pelosi agreed with Bernie. Really? Still? Women are the poorest of the poor across the globe. What is so difficult to see and understand?

For me, abortion is always steeped in controversy and also nonnegotiable. It is a policy that clarifies that certain issues will always assist in uncovering what "revolutionary" means. Hillary Clinton has claimed she wants abortion safe, legal, and rare. #Feminism4the99 demands full access to abortion in a world that must be egalitarian for each person. Make the world kind and equal and abortion will become a different kind of choice. But so-called prolife Democrats and Republicans are not trying to make the world kinder. They are legislating ways to punish the doctors who do abortions and the women who need them.

Misogyny may become less white as it becomes a tool for the majority Brown and Black globe. Abolitionist socialist feminists of every color must see that this does not happen. But let us not get ahead of ourselves; white masculinist men and heterosexist racists are still in charge, doing their deeds in belligerent ways.

As global capital attempts to find its footing in a changing world, nations sputter and struggle and more and more people are displaced and precarious. Millions of people—Syrians, Nigerians, Rohingya, Palestinians—become refugees, migrants, and displaced. People in crisis are on the move everywhere. Existing borders will become irrelevant given this human dilemma. And liberal and neoliberal democracy will be found wanting more than ever.

I want to underscore that neoliberal doctrine is not simply economic at its core. Neoliberalism developed initially as a backlash in the United States against the gains made by the women's and civil rights movements toward equality. Neoliberalism and the latest iteration of neoconservatism have argued since early in the 1970s that the US has become too equal, that expectations for gender and racial equality have become so expansive that there is no way that government can meet these demands. Global capitalism is solidifying and expressing new commitments.

Neoliberals believe that if one rolls back the expectations of what government can accomplish people will expect less and then the government will function much better. The downsizing and restructuring of both the government and people's expectations go hand-in-hand. Republicans today call this dismantling the administrative state. Shrinking national monuments and their public lands are part and parcel of this mentality. But remember that this backlash started with the gains of the civil rights and women's movements in the 1960s.

There are some foundational truths to be seen here. The US state is experiencing a crisis of majoritarian white supremacy and of the men and the structures that uphold it. Yet the old structural assists like the Electoral College, gerrymandering, and extralegal restrictions on voting are not yet gone, nor are the white men and women who fight to protect them. This is a reminder that plantation economies may end, yet the former slave master is able to extend his brutal power and privileges.

Historian Tera Hunter describes the fraught years after the Civil War when Black women struggled through the chaos of sharecropping, Reconstruction, Jim Crow, and post-slavery marriage laws. As Hunter shows, legal endings are very different than actual ones. The plantation economy did not need or want *slave* marriage; it wanted to claim all of black women's labor—including their progeny—as its own.

Thomas Jefferson spoke against slavery but owned slaves. He had an entire shadow family with Sally Hemings, one of the many slaves he owned, and gave his white daughter twenty-seven slaves as a wedding gift so that she would have an appropriate dowry. He instructed that "his" slaves should be given their freedom at the death of his wife, Martha, although this did not happen.

Dolley Madison, wife of James Madison, and mistress of his Virginia estate, acquired slaves through her marriage. Black slaves gave her social standing inside a patriarchal marriage system that gave her few rights in relation to her husband, but total rights in relation to her enslaved "help." Their lives were completely determined by her demands, her relocation after remarriage, etc.

The plantation economy eventually ended, but not the white misogynist and capitalist supremacy that drove it. Chattel slavery was an intimate weaving of class, sex, and race. Each of them is all of them. Similarly, Black men and women, though differently, are positioned in the newly evolving economy, free, but without their rights. This is the racist capitalist misogynist classic contradiction: to be free is not to be equal. We are living at the end of something but not quite with a new enough beginning.

If antiracist white women, enough of us, recognize this horrific legacy threaded through and alongside important legal gains and civil and women's rights struggles, then we can move beyond the myth of success. Barack Obama was the first Black president both because of all this and in spite of it.

Abolitionism—the abolition of white supremacist misogyny and its capitalist nexus alongside the racist misogyny of everyday practices—must become the heart of the visionary framework. If assimilation, reform, accommodation, integration, and equality presume the foundational structure of class, sex, race, and gender, then a new foundation must be imagined. We can start with a materialism of the body that is never singularly of any color, sex, gender, or bodily ability in a shared commons, rather than in a class hierarchy.

I continue to ponder and be enraged that a known and self-avowed sexual predator remains US president along with his coterie of known sexual harassing male appointees—free to terrorize so many of us and the globe. And that so many white women have assisted him in doing so.

How do antiracist feminists think about and mobilize in this moment that we inhabit? My comrade and antiviolence activist, Eve Ensler, asks, "how do you live at the edge of what is over?" I wonder with her, how do you know when something is really done? And how do you know how to use the leftover remains to complete the upheaval?

XIII. REVOLUTIONIZING #METOO, #TIMESUP, #USTOO, #SEXUALSPRING

Sexual abuse is ubiquitous to misogynist power. It thrives inside patriarchal racist privilege. The #MeToo movement, first named as such by activist Tarana Burke in 2007, exposed this reality, especially for girls of color. Differing forms of sexual harassment, from intimidation to rape, can appear in every crevice of life. And very often, the perpetrators are protected by silence and shaming.

It was not until white celebrities in the film industry began to use #MeToo that it became a national conversation. The exposure of Harvey Weinstein's sexual malice began the present wave of naming and outings of workplace sexual predators. More and more men were named and fell, so to speak. Weinstein has been dethroned and may end up in prison, but the long-term effect on ending sexual violence remains unknown.

Exposing rape is not the same as ending misogyny. Knowing is not the same as having power. Being informed can mobilize or deflect. The silences surrounding sexual violence complicate the response. But not knowing does not erase complicity. If I say I did not know, does that relieve me of my responsibility to act? Do people sometimes choose to not know and not act? If I know I must speak, but if I cannot, what is the effect? How do we make sure that we do not accept silence even while understanding why some people are silent?

Related problems for addressing the structural realities exist as well. Hollywood is not the same as the service industry, or prison complex, or where domestic workers, nannies, home health aides, house cleaners, and prisoners are regularly abused. Sexual molestation, harassment, discrimination, and violence are a problem wherever women's work is located.

The structural presence of male privilege and sexual violence applies everywhere. This is unquestionably *not* a singular, individual problem. I am aware of how risky it is to say "everywhere" or "always." But patriarchal racism is a universal hierarchical and punishing systemic power-granting and power-denying edifice. It is universal, although with particular stories. The hardest part to reckon with is that the structural edifice that powers racist sexual domination is so often made invisible, and/or mystified and unaccountable. In part, this is how the structure of patriarchy remains such an unrecognized force.

When women—cisgender or self-identified—argue that sexual violence is individual and structural simultaneously, it means that there is no personal solution to a political problem. What is the structural power that allows sexual violence? It has architecture and is designed to devalue and control through the inability to protect our bodies and our lives. The structure that underpins rape and sexual violence configures a female commodification that is systemic and systematic. The dynamic terrorizes, manipulates, and denigrates. At the same time, misogynist power can applaud and give recognition.

In this moment of #MeToo and #TimesUp it is crucial to see these violations as part of the larger political structuring of women within the sexual division of labor that violates their ability to secure a livelihood. Why not think of repairing sexual violence with a guaranteed minimum income for all, or a fifteen-dollar living wage, or reproductive justice and full access to health care and abortion, or entry into jobs that have not been easily available for women, or day care and parental leave that is not tied to a job?

It seems impossible to know what actually can make real change just now. But the work to be done begins by making these claims, together, for each other. Recognizing the constant connection between our individual lives and the power-filled structures of misogyny and racism and capitalism is a start. It is a real challenge to solidify a social justice #Feminism4the99. Mariame Kaba, founder of Project Nia, whose mission is to end youth incarceration, envisions a transformative justice that recognizes the deep connections between sexual violence, incarceration, mental illness, policing, poverty, and the misogyny that threads through it all.

At issue is the universal underpinning of power by sexual violation/harassment/rape as the manifestation of patriarchy in all its racist and colonialist/capitalist forms. The violation shames, intimidates, and punishes women. Silences must be ended in order to create collective, political, structural responses that can make enough of a difference.

Racist patriarchy cannot be reformed sufficiently to wipe out sexual violation and violence. The hierarchy of wealth and fame that encodes misogynist power and privilege will have to be toppled if sexual violence is to be fully challenged and eradicated. The individual commodification of our bodies along with every other dimension of ourselves must be reimagined. The hierarchy of white supremacy must be brought to an end. Sexual violation is a form of dehumanization that runs throughout the structures of capitalism—in the commitment to profit rather than human need; in the system of white domination where people of color suffer the dehumanization of discrimination.

Weinstein raped and molested hundreds of women. Bill Cosby drugged and raped over sixty of us. Larry Nassar violated over three hundred girls. This is more than individual hubris. The stunning numbers and repetition scream out for a power-filled redress. Tinkering with the system is not enough. The structures of sexual exploitation are irrepressible and seemingly unshakeable. Liberalism is insufficient because it protects the very foundation of racist patriarchy that needs dissolution. Again, reform is inadequate. We must have revolutionary goals.

#MeToo is a collective political expression used to expose the secrets that cover up the power systems. It should not be understood as simply an individual personal indictment of isolated stories. It needs to become a movement joined with other movements. Tarana Burke and many other activists remain committed to doing this.

#MeToo must extend to each war and its rape camps, from Rwanda to Bosnia to Syria to Myanmar to Palestine, and to the raped and trafficked Yazidi women. It must extend to each profession, each workplace, each prison, each detention center.

Sexual violation needs political status. It needs grounding in political vision to help guide and mobilize revolutionary attention. It needs to be understood as the putty that holds together the overlapping, codependent, violating, and comprehensive systems of dehumanization. Sexual violence is hard to resist. It makes it hard to live.

Today's iteration of #MeToo has developed in neoliberal America. It often suffers from a hyper-individualist and hyper-apolitical articulation. Our sights must be focused on the connection between the individual atrocities of sexual violation and their structural privilege. Otherwise individual men can be punished, but the hierarchy of cis/hetero/white privilege remains in place, possibly rejiggered for the moment. The individual stories that expose and connect the practices of racist misogyny that empower individual males is where we must mobilize.

Radical feminists of the late 1960s and 1970s were famous for their insight that the personal is political, that there is a politics to sex. But this insight has not fostered the revolutionary and structural assault that it so richly deserves. Too often the personal is reduced only to the political or the political to the personal, and an assault on the site where they interlock is hard to locate.

Given this, women are often implicated in the very oppressions that define us. I do not use this as a charge against, but rather as a recognition that each of us is embedded in the structures of power we inhabit and silence operates as protection.

I am eager to deal with the personal and the political, the individual and the structural. Individual and structural sites of power are always inhabited together; that is what makes fabulous antiracist anticapitalist feminist thinking so hard. It is part of *the* structural dilemma. And this structural dilemma is global.

Global capital most often rules with white men and they are ruling locales of the global economy rather than nation-states, as these locales once were known. The less economic borders matter, the more nationalism is constructed with renewed white supremacist racial and sexual identities.

Trump tries to fortify his support with white women despite his sexually predatory ways. It is primarily white women who do his bidding. Sarah Huckabee Sanders, as Trump's press secretary, lies to the public daily; Nikki Haley, the former US ambassador to the UN, was an apologist for Zionism and the slaughter and massacre of peaceful demonstrators by Israeli defense forces; Gina Haspel, the CIA director, at first defended torture and then under pressure said it was a mistake, but not morally reprehensible; education secretary Betsy DeVos knows little of public schools and is not interested anyway; Melania Trump pretends to be his wife; Ivanka Trump pretends to be a feminist.

White female bodies can oversee misogyny and deny the 99 percent of women their agency. It is more important than ever to expunge the sexual violence that protects all this. Becoming a part of the existing structure is not a liberatory strategy. Reforms that have the potential to be abolitionist and revolutionary must be the guide.

XIV. FRAMING ABOLITIONISM

Abolition demands radical and revolutionary commitments. It means going to the root and following the nexus of routes that allow the present heterocapitalist, white-supremacist, misogynist, able-bodied patriarchy to enforce the binaries of rich and poor, white and colored, disabled and abled, cis and trans.

Abolitionism is an interlocking, radically inclusive, multilayered politics of revolutionary imaginings. I continue to wonder what keeps misogyny from becoming a cite of/for abolition? Why is the sexual violence of misogyny, both in families and in wars, the best-kept open secret of them all? Is it because girls and women of each and every race are men's wives, sisters, daughters, aunts, and grandmothers? Maybe it is the intimacy that provides cover for this formidable, oppressive structuring of power.

I keep finding new forms of complicity within the systems of racism and class privilege. Our abolitionist feminism must commit to *abolishing* each form of racial and sexual violence along with the hierarchies of economic class and heteropatriarchy in their white privileged forms. This process of both seeing and dismantling is, and maybe will always be, incomplete and ongoing.

I am not sure James Baldwin is nuanced enough when he says that being white is an attitude more than a color, that you are as white as you think you are and therefore whiteness is a choice, but that for Blacks their color is a "condition" and not a choice. But I like the lack of equivalence, making whiteness a choice, showing that whites have an added responsibility for the times "we" *all* live in. What does this mean for white antiracist abolitionist socialist feminists? It means our silence and avoidance and hesitancy to confront is not allowed. There is no middle ground. There is no compromise.

This recognition happened for me a long time ago, while working alongside my Black feminist friends, when the white mainstream mid-1970s women's movement was openly and doggedly indicted for its racism. My friendship with Gloria Watkins, a.k.a. bell hooks, was critical to me in this period.

I must challenge my privilege and not be/act white and use this privilege of choice to help make a revolution that is structural but also a personal affair. If Frantz Fanon and truth-telling author Frank Wilderson are right, and white people function in their own corporeality as deputies of the state, this unauthorized *deputization* must be destroyed._

I use the phrase *newest–new* racism to highlight the fact that violence towards Blacks and people of color has a too-long history. The *newest-new* racism replaces homogeneity with complexity, fluidity, and the modernization of the slave relation itself. Black slavery, as Professor Saidiya Hartman describes it, was the ultimate form of dehumanization, severing people from their families, especially their mothers, and their sense of place. Today's racism is no longer articulated in an actual system of chattel slavery but is instead enforced through a prison/police state of carceral punishment that has shattering likenesses to slavery itself.

White dominance makes being Black irreconcilable with safety and opportunity for most. Afro-pessimists like Wilderson describe the continual dispossession of Black life. Jared Sexton, another major thinker about modern Black life, calls this hatred of Blackness "captive flesh," and literary critic Hortense Spillers writes of the Black woman's body as a "hieroglyphics of the flesh." And yet Blackness also remains defiant today in the resistance of movements like Black Lives Matter and #SayHerName.

Saidiya Hartman writes that she is living in "an afterlife of slavery" and in a "future created by" slavery. She asks us to remember that "the present was created by people in chains" so that "slavery feels proximate rather than remote." Freddie Gray's killing by Baltimore police harkens back to this past. His neck was broken. He was killed having had neither a trial nor a jury. It was an execution of sorts. State prosecutor Marilyn Mosby determined that the arrest was illegal at the start. Former Black Panther Eddie Conway says that the police were a mob carrying out a modern-day lynching.

Slavery exists in its *new-old* and *newest-new* forms in the prison system, as decarceration activists Angela Davis and Ruthie Gilmore have argued for decades. They have shown the carceral system to be the backbone of today's racism. It infiltrates the daily life of a majority of Blacks through its invasive metrics. Black captive bodies reside inside and outside the penal state in its modern form.

These newer kinds of slavery and lynching have been put in view by the Equal Justice Initiative led by the insurgent lawyer/activist Bryan Stevenson. In an exhibit at the Brooklyn Museum, the Initiative used artworks and archival material to document how lynching has moved from outside on trees to inside to the electric chair. I visited the Legacy Museum and Lynching Memorial in Montgomery, Alabama, to be reminded of the atrocities Black Americans have lived with for centuries.

The spate of publicized police murders of young Black men has again exposed the murderous violence of white supremacy. This publicizing should connect us back to earlier viciousness toward Abner Louima, Rodney King, and the Black teenagers falsely incarcerated for rape in the Central Park Five case. It is well known by now that Trump called for their execution at the time. It took years for them to be found innocent.

And we should not be allowed to forget the life of Kalief Browder, a Black teenager jailed for three years without a trial in New York's Rikers Island jail, where he was beaten and frequently kept in solitary confinement. He was arrested for stealing a backpack. He refused plea bargains because he said he was innocent. He languished imprisoned for three years because he stood by his innocence, while his jailers abused him repeatedly. When his case was finally resolved and Kalief was released from Rikers Island, he was unable to cope with all that had happened to him while jailed. He killed himself shortly thereafter.

Many hoped there would be a new accountability and transparency with a Black president, as well as with new technological capacity such as cell phone cameras that could capture police violations. But Obama sided with the rule of law even when it seemed unfair, as depicted in the film *Whose Streets?*, about the killing of Michael Brown and the ensuing Ferguson uprising. And surveillance cameras have done little to create accountability for police brutality. This was once again evident in the acquittal of Jason Stockley, the white officer who shot an unarmed Black man in St. Louis, Missouri. A white officer who killed a Black man in an unprovoked attack faced no consequences. The streets of St. Louis were filled with protestors in scenes reminiscent of Ferguson.

I wonder how Audre Lorde would update her insight about the "master's tools" in today's world. The leadership of Black Lives Matter, Million Hoodies, Hands Up United, Dream Defenders, to name a few, is staffed with people of all genders and sexual orientations, creating a more varied collective of resisters. Both racism and antiracist activists have become more varied.

White antiracist feminists must not allow nor choose our own white privilege but should be close, really close—in neighborhoods, schools, parks, restaurants, and everywhere—to Black and Brown lives, each one, that always matter. We must be ready to attack racism and misogyny by first redistributing white wealth through a tax or other system of reparations that will rebuild infrastructures that benefit everyday life in communities of color.

With abolition, whiteness would be a distinction without a difference, an identity without privilege. If white supremacy were to be truly dismantled, nothing should be left of whiteness. I remain hopeful along with historian Nell Painter, who tells us that there is no such thing as a white race. There is so much left to be done.

XV. ON BUILDING REVOLUTIONARY CONNECTORS

I write in the hopes of weaving together civil rights, disability rights, indigenous people's rights, and sex, gender, economic, immigrant, refugee, and environmental justice movements. The need for connection emerges out of the truth that no one resistance is enough. And that the crises the planet faces are too many and interrelated: climate disaster alone, with its punishing and killing floods and tsunamis and typhoons, wreaks havoc. The poorest of the globe suffer the most. And these poor are disproportionately women and their children.

But in the US, alongside the crisis of the planet, exist the trauma of health care and the ferocity of the carceral state, most especially if you are Black, Brown, or an undocumented immigrant. Building liaisons between movements at their points of shared contact is crucial. My method for seeing how to do this is to look at the multiplicities of any one self, to look across sex, class, race, gender, to lay the potential of this collective activism.

Emmett Till was murdered at the age of fourteen in 1955 on the false claim of raping a white woman. In 1964, white civil rights workers James Chaney, Mickey Schwerner, and Andrew Goodman were murdered by the KKK. Fred Hampton of the Black Panthers was shot and killed by Chicago police in 1969. Rodney King, a Black Angeleno, was brutalized by white police in 1991. Abner Louima was sodomized with a broken-off broom handle by white New York police officers. Color trumps class. He had been an electrical engineer in Haiti before coming to the United States. There is a structural story here for coalitional work to address.

Amidst the violence of today, Black Lives Matter has emerged, with its many dispersed organizations and actions. The Black Lives Matter and Hands Up, Don't Shoot movements continue the struggle to dismantle and abolish racial hatred in the structural leftovers of economic and gender inequality. The Movement for Black Lives, a policy collective representing Black people throughout the United States, reorients, redirects, and condemns the white gaze and its punishing hands. It demands a revolutionary assault on white supremacy.

What would it look like to annihilate racism, as B. R. Ambedkar, the Indian Dalit writer and activist, asks? The activists of Black Lives Matter ponder these questions and employ new tactics to make change. Their demonstrations are spontaneous and localized, but they are also unified. They are making a new movement for racial justice that imbibes the intersectional connections of sex, race, and class divisions.

It is important that Obama served as president because it shows that an individual Black man cannot redress the problem of racism. Racism is not an individual problem, and no one individual can fix it even if they want to. The structures themselves corrupt and coopt, so the commitments must be revolutionary.

Black Lives Matter activists disrupt the systems that support racism from outside established quarters. They use disruption to expose the injustice and use exposure of the injustice to disrupt. They will stay in the streets till police officers are held accountable and Dick Cheney and his gang are found guilty of war crimes and Palestine is free. For BLM, liberation struggles are international and global. At the start of their US activism they traveled to Palestine to establish an international connection between freedom struggles. For them the fight for self-determination knows no national borders: from chattel slave trade to the Palestinian liberation struggle.

When people work across differences, we can at least temporarily move beyond the limits of division. Unity is not the end goal here, but a complex and variegated solidarity of all people of color, nonimmigrant and immigrant, refugee and nonrefugee, indigenous, Black, LatinX, Native, trans, disabled, and Muslim. Build the connectors between each of these with their sex, race, and class dimensions.

Connectors allow for solidarity with and between the differences. Coalitional politics recognizes multiple but shared aims. Political organizing must move beyond the categories that push us apart to a solidarity that is strengthened by its internal tensions.

This is a moment for cross-movement and intersecting actions that create new alliances that might not be known or even imagined yet. This means supporting autonomous actions that become cross movement through the intersections that exist within each demand. Until the work continues it is impossible to know what kind of new alliances can be formed.

BYP100 (Black Youth Project); Black Lives Matter; Moral Mondays, a grassroots antiracism movement in North Carolina led by Rev. William Barber; #SayHer-Name; SURJ (Standing Up for Racial Justice); Mass Freedom, a project to join movements to end criminalization of people of color; Chicago Teachers Union (CTU); National Disability Rights Network; White Coats for Black Lives, which seeks to dismantle racism in medicine; Fight for $15; ROC (Restaurant Opportunities Centers) United; OUR (Organization United for Respect) at Walmart;

March 8 International Women's Strike; Women's March; the R3 (Resist, Reimagine, Rebuild) coalition in Chicago; #DAPL (Dakota Access Pipeline activists); Code Pink, a women-led international human rights group; Jewish Voice for Peace; the March for Black Women (#M4BW); #Feminism4the99; 100 Women of Color; the Resistance Schools at Harvard and Berkeley; Black Women's Blueprint; People's Congress of Resistance, convening grassroots groups from across the country; groups fighting for LGBTQIA and indigenous land rights—these are just a few of the thousands of resistance groups in the US today.

The Beyond the Moment campaign, initiated by the national Black Lives Matter network and their partners, called for May 1, 2017, to be a day to stand up against the Immigration and Customs Enforcement (ICE) raids and to demand worker's rights, especially for immigrant and undocumented workers. Black and Brown people, immigrant communities, the economically unstable, women, children, the disabled, the LGBTQIA community, those working to protect our right to work and those fighting for our right to clean air and water, are all facing attacks because of a minority whose values are rooted in capitalist-misogynist white supremacy.

A movement of movements recognizes and allows for complex interweavings that recognize people's double-jeopardy and adverse specificity, It also allows for people's multiple status, bothness, and allness, to flourish. It is not enough to say that sex, class, and race overlap with each other. They rather structure the selves and practices that already have multiple expressions.

We are connected *and* divided by the threads of sexism, racism, white privilege, militarism, environmental degradation, ableism, heterosexism, and transphobia. Sexist and racist violence oppresses so many of us, most especially women of color, Native, and immigrant women. There is a possible complex intermixed camaraderie in the making here.

The work must commit to being radically sweeping and fully encompassing. When one thinks of protecting the earth and climate, this requires naming environmental racism and environmental sexism as the hazards that they are. Robert Bullard, often described as the father of environmental justice, reiterates that people do not suffer in the same way from the climate disaster we all face: people of color live in areas that are the most at risk here and abroad. Mary Robinson, the former president of Ireland, has been a leader in the climate movement for decades. She says that things have so worsened that ignoring the looming catastrophe for the most vulnerable is unconscionable.

Women, especially disabled women of color, face particular challenges as hurricanes hit, as was so clear with Hurricane Katrina more than a decade ago. Yet Katrina is often explained as exposing racism and poverty, ignoring the impact on women, even though pictures of women and children evacuated to the Superdome were frequently on view. And, 150,000 Katrina exiles found themselves in Houston as Hurricane Harvey hit. Race and gender, with class, define the particular vulnerability of climate risk today.

Poor people of every color face the misery of drought, of floods, and tsunamis in more calamitous fashion than others, and poor people come in every sex, gender, sexual orientation, bodily ability, and geographic location. Climate change amplifies these disparities, so the resolution of these crises must address these inequities.

Bombs and missiles (their manufacture and the damage they wreak) heat the globe. One cannot support the wars in Syria, Iraq, Afghanistan, Gaza, and Yemen without endangering human existence around the globe. We must end militarism and war to cool the earth and end violence of every kind. An antiracist, antimilitarist/imperialist, antimisogynist climate justice demands that differences are recognized in order to find the huge commonality needed to save each of us, and with us, the planet. Indigenous women, especially in the global South have long been at the forefront of eco-socialism.

After forty years of antiracist, feminist, socialist activism and writing, I yearn for more meaningful change toward this world I try to imagine. Most of my radical friends, whether working inside or outside electoral and alternative politics, also hope for more. This was true of the gathering I attended of many progressive groups held shortly after Trump's victory.

The meeting, representing approximately forty different resistance groups and activists, was held in Stone Ridge, New York. We met to strategize on how to support each other, a mixed racial and gender group of progressives who were socialist feminists and antiviolence feminists, leaders from environmental justice and climate change groups, Black activists, Native activists from North Dakota, leaders in the fights for disability rights, prison reform and abolition, and Palestinian rights. We named ourselves *A Movement of Movements* and committed ourselves to supporting each other and the many resistance groups we represented, with newly forming assemblages.

This new radical camaraderie also emerged in the work I did as part of the organizing committee of the International Women's Strike/US on May 8, 2017. This was the first time in a very long while that feminists of the left in the United States came together as different kinds of socialists to demand a feminism that works for most women, a #Feminism4the99. I had not worked with the Black feminist activist and writer Barbara Smith since our early friendship when she was writing the Combahee River Collective statement.

The US organizing committee was led by Professors Tithi Bhattacharya and Cinzia Arruzza, who directed our

coalition of multiple socialist feminist groups committed to ending women's exploitation and the oppression of
wage-earning/nonwage-earning women, women of color,
Native women, and so many others. The International
Women's Strike/US committed to organizing women in
all the varieties of labor that they do, breaking the borders between the wage economy and the home, between
public and private life. The organizing spread throughout
much of the United States with large demonstrations in
New York City and Los Angeles. These friends and political networks are a source of much of the sustenance I rely
on for what I write here, in this disheartening time. By
now there are thousands of protest groups and organizations that are deeply committed to ongoing resistance to
and disruption of Trump's agenda.

Upon Trump's victory, resisters, protectors, and protestors warned that we should not *normalize* anything
about his regime. And now it may be time to say that
resisters should not *normalize* resistance itself. In the last
many months of protest in 2018, as Trump continued to
flail and tweet and enact horrifically punishing initiatives,
it became clearer that resistance is simply not enough.
More formidable disruption and defiance is needed, even
if we do not know what this exactly looks like.

Immediately after Trump's election, the massive
marches and continuous outcry by so many in the resistance—against the travel bans, the forced deportations,

the Dakota Access Pipeline, the attacks on Planned Parenthood, the assaults on poor people and Obamacare, the climate change denial—was invigorating. The millions who poured onto the streets for the Women's March the day after the inauguration, the tens of thousands who stood in defiance of the travel ban in our airports, encouraged and created needed disruption. The Trump election had awakened us.

But outrageous policy continues to be made. Trump lurches forward with new and old wars fueled by his clueless arrogance and hubris. He pretends he is speaking for coal miners, but many coal miners have not claimed him. Many of them actually say that they want good jobs, not outdated, poor paying, and dangerous ones. An important *fact:* the United Mine Workers never endorsed Trump. Indeed, Trump has filled the Department of Labor with anti-labor lobbyists and anti-union corporate executives.

Trump says he cares about the "dreamers" and then ends DACA (Deferred Action for Childhood Arrivals) for eight hundred thousand young people whose lives are torn asunder by his racist and nationalist moorings. Next, he appears to have made a deal with the Democrats to find a legal way forward for these young people. Each day brings a new tweet, but no affirmative coherent policy. Instead his incoherence intensifies the cruelty of many of his policies.

Next, Trump revoked the temporary protected status for Haitians, Salvadorans, and Hondurans, most of them immigrants who have lived in the United States for decades, have jobs, and pay taxes. These revocations were expected to affect 273,000 American-born children, potentially separating them from their parents.

Trump declared a zero-tolerance immigration policy that further criminalizes asylum seekers and all migrants from Mexico and Central and South America. All the while his properties have hired undocumented, mainly women, workers. The deportations and family separations have exacerbated the latest intolerable and unconscionable carceral system where children are detained in prison-like cages. The suffering for these families is immense, the consequences heartbreaking.

XVI. CREATING REVOLUTIONARY POSSIBILITIES

I want to burst the boundaries of socialism with radical feminisms, and the boundaries of feminisms with anti-racist socialism, and the boundaries of abolitionism with a queer feminism. Imagining that through these avenues we can find new revolutionary strategies.

The ruthless brutality of white privilege embedded and reproduced in settler colonialism and then in slavery gestates in every crevice of this country. It is the dirty open secret that repeats itself in new forms of injustice through dispossession and humiliation. Abolition and revolution are the only lasting remedy.

There is too much hunger and homelessness and illness and unhappiness and war and loneliness and desperation and fleeing and loss. There is a better way. I am thinking that more and more people across this globe know this.

And more and more people in the United States do as well. It is why the politicians are becoming more punishing and vile. So right-wing governments seek to quell resistance, and also instigate support for their regimes while doing so. Trying to educate and mobilize for and with an abolitionist socialist feminism remains a huge challenge. Yet I believe that the cruel present conditions we are experiencing demand liberation struggles. And, without imagining them they can never come into being.

Economic inequality is at obscene and unconscionable levels. White supremacy continues to be murderous to people of color. Islamophobia and anti-immigrant policies create impossible lives. Hurricanes Katrina and Harvey and Irma and Maria were not simply natural disasters. The suffering of Puerto Rico, along with the Caribbean in general, must be on the immediate political agenda. These are white-man-made, capitalist climate disasters. Those who suffer the most in these storms are the least responsible for the havoc. The injustice of all this is truly catastrophic. The time is now.

Because white supremacy is not a stand-alone system, if you are committed to ending the climate catastrophe of the planet, make sure to target the environmental racism of this misery. If you are committed to fighting for reproductive justice, make sure you focus on making contraception and abortion accessible and safe for *all* women. If you believe in land rights for indigenous peoples, make clear that indigenous women must live free of sexual violence. If you stand for single-payer health care, demand an end to pharmaceutical excess. Make your commitment plural and without exception. Build a revolutionary stance with this.

From Occupy to the Moral Monday protests to Ferguson to Gaza to the People's Climate March in 2014, we all must move forward together. Revolutionary possibility is located here, building a movement of our movements, a fusion of our differences, solidarity from and with our particularities.

The modernized tyranny and brutality of the US state and its collaboration with transnational corporations requires brilliance on our part to thwart the confines that it attempts to imprison most of us within. Do not look for a revolution like those of the past. We need one for the future, one that is accountable to the people who have *unfairly* suffered the most. Those who have suffered the most must guide and lead.

Resistance is not enough. Reform is not enough. Civil rights are not enough. Women's rights are not enough. In other words: liberalism and liberal feminism do not work for this moment, if they ever did. Abolition is our necessary revolutionary method. But it remains to find out how to imagine the *new* in revolutionary ways.

Moderation and moderates, especially white moderates, are not the solution. Moderation may just be the greatest challenge today. A group of Black religious leaders wrote in a *New York Times* op-ed that white moderates know things have to change but worry too much about their own sense of comfort and safety, just as they did throughout the 1960s, when most white liberals did not support civil rights protests or Martin Luther King. If you are waiting for a perfect moment or protest, it does not exist. The civil rights movement was much messier and more disorderly and sometimes violent than it is often depicted. The time *is now*, even if it does not feel like it is.

Systems of power do not erode all at once. They do so in fits and starts and with repetitions and they never collapse simply on their own. But there are moments when political structures are more vulnerable than others. I am thinking this is one such moment, a moment of singularity further intensified and exposed by climate disasters and their challenges that also make us brave. I am hoping this is so.

Black women leaders like the Black Lives Matter founders call forth the Black body as a site for universal justice. As BLM cofounder Alicia Garza says, when Black people really get free, then *every single person in this world has a better shot at getting and staying free.* Farah Tanis, cofounder of Black Women's Blueprint and organizer of the March for Black Women in 2017, has put Black women in the bold in the fight against racism.

It is from the site of Black and Brown and LatinX female bodies that the exclusionary history of universalism is fully delegitimized. This remedy needs constant remembering: false (white) universals obscure the fact that nonspecificity is a mask for injustice. Abstract individuals presume whiteness and maleness. Specifying the individual by gender and race and color creates a newly-inclusive site for democratic demands. It is time to try things this way after so much of history has been blinded by exclusionary rights parading as inclusive and just.

When Frank Rich asked Chris Rock if the election of Barack Obama meant progress, Rock said, yes, it showed progress for white people. They were the ones with the problem, not Black people, who were and always have been ready to have a Black president. Rock said his children were meeting the nicest white people that America has ever produced. Let us require that antiracist whites can keep producing nicer white people.

I will take Chris Rock's optimism and try to put it to good use, but I am also reminded of Frantz Fanon's statement: "We revolt simply because, for many reasons, we can no longer breathe." Be reminded of Eric Garner pleading for his life, saying "I can't breathe" eleven times before he died.

Now that there has been a Black president, a Black woman secretary of state, a Black attorney general, a Black Joint Chief of Staff, a Black woman commander of the Army's elite drill sergeant school, we know such changes are insufficient for liberation.. There is an evolving militarized police state that orchestrates an unforgiving racism that continues to put Black bodies of all genders at risk while also diversifying this racism with Black bodies. Complexity should not be misread as fundamental change. It instead reveals modern racist misogyny in its disparate heterogeneity.

Organizing will continue with priorities shifting and coalescing because of the overlap among differing demands for change. If we use the method of abolitionist socialist feminism to see the pluralism within health care for all or #MeToo or reproductive justice, our shared purpose will direct this intersectional struggle. This work demands trust and love as we try to go forward together.

There will be fractious and disturbing arguments and conflicts. But these moments are opportunities to negotiate our differences such that these conversations become key building blocks of insurgency. New unknown alliances and possibilities will emerge from these struggles. Individuals will need to begin before they know that they are ready. These collective actions will express the readiness that is needed.

Yes, the next strategies are unclear, but I think the massive numbers of people and groups that are already resisting are beginning the process of building revolutionary actions. People of color and antiracist whites build new possibilities. There are thousands of groups resisting right-wing misogynist white supremacy today and it is time to connect and publicize ourselves to each other. Maybe a massive shutdown of everyday life in the US could assist this visibility. Remember, right-wing takeovers are most often done by the few, not the many.

The collective power of progressive movements needs visibility. Acts of civil disobedience are growing. Activist filmmaker Bree Newsome scaled a flagpole to bring down the South Carolina Confederate flag. Black Lives Matter has led demonstrations that repeatedly closed down highways. Some six hundred women were arrested in Washington, D.C., for protesting immigrant childhood detention. Activist Therese Patricia Okoumou climbed the Statue of Liberty to protest the caging of these immigrant children who have been seized from their parents.

Next steps will involve public actions at our workplaces and as consumers and in recognizing transnational alliances. A few of the many groups already doing this kind of work (and not yet mentioned) are: Project South dedicated to the elimination of poverty and genocide; the pro-Immigrant Cosecha Movement; the National Domestic Workers Alliance; the Never Again antigun student movement; Mijente, the proLatinX, Black, and queer #FreeOurFuture movement.

People can coalesce around the many demands already in play, such as single-payer affordable healthcare for all; alternatives to, and abolition of, prisons; a universal guaranteed income; full access to contraception and abortion; zero carbon emissions starting now; universal and publicly funded quality childcare and early education programs; the end of massive military spending, with monies redirected to infrastructure and housing; justice and freedom for Palestine; banning the use of fossil fuels, including a ban on fracking; affordable housing for all; stopping detentions of immigrants, defending immigrant rights, and expanding sanctuary cities; full accessibility for disabled people; land rights for indigenous people; reparations to Black and Native communities; ending the colonization of Puerto Rico.

There are still many other related initiatives: housing justice; clean water for Flint, Michigan; an end to voter suppression; equal pay for equal work; protection of sexual health; a fifteen-dollar minimum wage; paid family leave; LGBTQIA justice; affordable college education; renewable energy development; recognition of tribal nations' rights; avoiding proxy wars at all costs. Connecting these issues while fighting for them furthers the process of making a revolution from the ground up.

People can be located in their particular struggles while forging new connections between movements. Working toward these listed commitments will begin to shift and change millions of people's lives. These policy initiatives are not sufficient in and of themselves, but they begin and continue the process toward racial, gender, and economic justice. History is always mapping new possibilities if we can just see them and seize them. Our lived lives can continue to radicalize us.

Revolution is a process. It is not a moment. Nor is it a *thing*, as in one event. The wide swath progressive peoples have cut through the culture can further develop cross-movement relationships that will build a revolutionary solidarity. Hopefully people will begin work stoppages of all sorts: as workers, as consumers, as parents, as nannies, etc., and recombine in a series of massive actions.

Revolutionary change may feel impossible but a politics of the seemingly impossible is needed more than ever. As a white antiracist, I caution white women and white antiracist feminists to make sure to confront our whiteness and its imperial privilege. Living in the heart of empire we must be very careful to never forget this. My guide, from the global feminist anti-violence activist group One Billion Rising, is: listen, disrupt, and connect.

The promise of the many women's marches since Trump was elected—often women of color–led, but primarily white—is of a movement that can be inclusive and loving. Antiracist white feminists must hold ourselves accountable to this vision. The signs held and the statements of the marchers speak of an enormous promise. When asked why they march, women across the country respond in numerous ways: for equality for everyone; for civil rights; for transgender rights; for Palestine; for immigrants; for refugees; for everyone; for Trayvon Martin; for everything; for women all over the world; for women with disabilities; for seeing and knowing more than I do now; for our bodies, for our reproductive rights; for the Rohingya; for Puerto Rico; for so many things; for the earth; for love and kindness.

Yet white antiracists must remain vigilant. Imperial white feminism remains a problem. It is a feminism that operates on behalf of US empire building. It has a history of using the Western canon of women's rights to justify US wars, most recently in Iraq, Afghanistan, and Syria. It imposes rather than negotiates. It dominates rather than liberates. It declares itself the exceptional arbiter of women's needs. It operates on behalf of the hierarchies of class across the globe, leaving most women out of the mix. It is not a #Feminism4the99.

I am reminded of my friend Nawal el Saadawi's response to a question at a teach-in in New York City just after the 2011 Egyptian uprising in Tahrir Square. Saadawi, a noted Egyptian feminist, was asked what people in the US could do to support revolution in Egypt "Make your own revolution and change your government for us," she answered.

I am hoping that people are ready to finally begin the complex abolitionist socialist feminist revolution that is

ABOLITIONIST SOCIALIST FEMINISM

needed. This feminism can never be too inclusive or too democratic. It will continue to be expansive, including those who are now most invisible. We must act with our communities, our families, our planet, and thus ourselves, against a thieving, militarized, corporate power structure. Apartheid conditions, wherever they exist, most especially in Palestine, have become the challenge of this century. Every form of sexual abuse and violence must be finally targeted and ended.

Women of each color already lead the fifteen-dollar-an-hour movement; Native women led the Standing Rock and Dakota Access Pipeline resistance; women of color led many of the climate disaster mobilizations and antipolice violence initiatives. Imagine if there was no rape, no incest, no sexual battery, or sexual violence of any and all sorts, how much more women could do. They would be free to love themselves and others, with no shame or fear or blame, and take this energy elsewhere.

If this violence were removed from the planet, along with the violence of exploitation, the globe could know peace. Flip and enlarge your vision. Make a revolution and free everybody's body from every form of violence. Take a stand. There is no middle ground left. Trump's minions are not bountiful enough. I am so ready. I know so very many people who are ready. It is time.

I do not know what the world will feel like with the abolition of white supremacy and misogyny and capitalism. But it is time to find out, for all of us. People of color have been ready since the start. As Black Lives Matter comrades chanted in the streets of Ferguson, Missouri, after Michael Brown was killed:

> *It is our duty to fight for our freedom.*
> *It is our duty to win.*
> *We must love and support one another.*
> *We have nothing to lose but our chains.*

Leave your sectarianism at home. Leave your purity there as well.

I am not sure of much except that *it is time*.

I am counting on my belief that enough of us are ready to be revolutionaries. We cannot know until we fully try.

Let us demand and originate the changes needed. As we do this together with each other, we will build the communities that we need and create a newly-found humanity.

We will find a name for this revolution where everyone can breathe. It is the revolution of all of our daughters and our willing sons, in all their glorious colors. They will make sure that this world is whole and just. They will make sure that children no longer pay the price for wars everywhere, will no longer be caged here in the US, alone, merely for crossing borders. I am ready for them.

XVII. A FEW AFTERTHOUGHTS

I completed the writing of this book several months before the 2018 midterm elections. Since then, much has happened. Trump has perfected his intersectional approach of hate and fear-mongering. He has honed his nationalist/misogynist/xenophobic racism in his continual assault against the Central American migrant caravan as criminals and invaders. And too many white women are still voting Republican. Many, especially in Texas, Georgia, and Florida, chose to support white supremacy.

Trump has amped up his nastiness, especially toward Black women journalists. He demonizes everyone but white men and their shared vision of America, promising no one else will be allowed entry. As I write, there are five thousand military troops camped out in tents along the southern border of the United States, waiting for the immigrant caravan.

The midterms were all about Trump. The 2018 election became a referendum that demanded a win for the

Democrats. No matter how many differences one had with the Dems, no matter how much one wondered if getting out the vote was enough or could work, most people who were part of the resistance to Trump had little choice. But was it enough?

How much longer will critics keep trying to make democracy democratic? Is it possible to overcome the electoral structure favoring largely white rural communities? Can any level of voter turnout negate the consequences of gerrymandered districts that privilege Republican voters? Can the Senate, structured as it is, ever allow fair representation as defined by one person, one vote? How can the Electoral College, as a remnant of slavery and government's deference to slave states, ever be made fair? Never has the electoral arena been exposed as clearly as in 2018 for its fraudulence, which is different than saying that this fraud is anything new.

The results are promising. The blue wave that early on looked pale blue, materialized into a formidable wave with large gains for Dems in the House. Record numbers of women won: 131 women are now in Congress. Two of the women elected are Indigenous, and two are Muslim, one a Somali immigrant. The first woman ever to be elected to the Senate from Arizona now sits in Congress, and she is bisexual. Florida passed Amendment Four, allowing 1.5 million former felons to be eligible to vote. That just might turn Florida blue in 2020.

These are amazing firsts, but it remains to be seen how much they matter. As I am completing this writing, Stacey Abrams ended her battle to become governor of Georgia by accepting that Brian Kemp would hold the seat, but she made clear that she would not concede an unfair election that included voter tampering, vote purging and suppression, lack of access, closed polling stations, and many more egregious acts. Looks like a neo-Confederacy in Georgia to me.

So whose democracy is this anyway? Trump Republicans no longer see democracy—in any guise, liberal or neoliberal—as viable for supporting their minority status. They opt instead for what Bertram Gross, a presidential advisor during Franklin Roosevelt's tenure, called "friendly fascism." The Supreme Court confirmation hearings of Brett Kavanaugh sealed the deal. Men are allowed to assault women and lie about it with no consequence. They can become Supreme Court justices, like Clarence Thomas and Kavanaugh. Our ill-conceived democracy crawled forward, but in shambles.

I think the country continues to edge toward a critical moment post-2018, or a singular moment. Democracy—neither liberal nor neoliberal—works well enough for many people. But as economic inequality reaches new heights, as racial discord and brutality are amplified, as misogyny is blasted over the airwaves, it becomes clearer to more people that they are the excluded ones, the ones being left out.

As there are more people wanting and needing their rights, as people of color increase their numbers, Black women especially, we must demand the democracy promised to each of us. Maybe it is not enough to declare historic first times anymore. Maybe the promise of justice has met its match with these new populations and their demands. Or maybe activists are just allowing the evolution and modernization of misogynist racist heteropatriarchy toward more equity, while never achieving equality and freedom.

Voting is not enough, if the very practice of voting is unequal and racist. Revolutionary reforms of the voting system must be enacted for us to make real progress toward racial, sexual, and class justice for our everyday lives.

Maybe some of the new radical women of color among the Democrats, like Alexandria Ocasio-Cortez and Ayanna Pressley, will initiate revolutionary reforms like abolishing the Electoral College along with the present representational structure of the Senate. Both are rooted in the needs of chattel slavery. If the focus for 2020 is a mobilized progressive vote, then make electronic voting secure and available to all. Election Day should be a holiday, a day off from work. Create the accessibility needed for democratic voting, which is not one and the same with democracy. Hopefully, out of this work, we can find our way to making everyday life participatory and radically free and equal.

I have one other critical realization to share about 2018, given my commitments. I wrote a book titled *The Radical Future of Liberal Feminism* in 1981. I argued that the conflicts between patriarchal racism and women's rights were so fraught that liberal feminism would radicalize itself. But I did not give enough recognition to the white supremacist commitments of many white and liberal, not to mention right-wing, women. Instead, many white women, when given a choice, have chosen to protect their own interest in their whiteness even though it is steeped in patriarchy. As such, these women have continued to support racist patriarchy.

In 2018, like 2016, white women in several key states like Georgia and Florida disproportionately voted for the Republican candidate. It seemed unfathomable to me that 52 percent of the women who voted in the governor's race in Georgia voted for Brian Kemp, and *not* Stacey Abrams. How is this possible? What were they thinking? They were thinking of their own white vulnerability and so-called safety instead.

White women who voted for Republicans, and earlier for Trump, voted for their whiteness over and above their other identities. Their class and sex and gender and race were "trumped" by white supremacy. For many white women, class does not trump race; gender does not trump race either. White women have historically supported racism and its misogyny too often. There are too many white women who are right wing and racist, and *not* feminist. Historically, white women married to slave-owning plantation men acceded to the brutality of slavery. They enjoyed their white economic privilege. They turned their heads and pretended to not see or know of the continued rape of enslaved women. They often were in the lynching mobs. Let us not forget GOP Mississippi senator Cindy Hyde-Smith who won her seat after saying that she would readily attend a public hanging and be in the front row. White women have allowed and supported violent, egregious, brutal racist practices. And today they too often do not stand up for Black women when they are being sidelined, silenced, ignored, or dehumanized.

Nevertheless, educated suburban women appear to have moved toward the Democrats in many of the 2018 elections. Educated and suburban as a description of women is shorthand for middle- and upper-middle-class white women. So maybe it is possible that class and gender will combine in this particular scenario to create a vote against Trump, and inadvertently, a vote against racism in 2020. Clearly, a mobilization of the complex and multiple and intersectional identities of women is key here.

As a white antiracist feminist I feel deeply the challenge to tackle white women's betrayal of women of color, especially Black women. This means targeting white women voters, encouraging them to reject white supremacy and its misogyny. But this is not enough, because to the extent people think that they are voting their interests, they defend their stance. That is why antiracist white women need to also work toward revolutionary reforms that will initiate new cross-racial alliances while undermining Trumpist rhetoric.

In the meantime, white antiracist women must understand that there is no white women's solidarity; there is no homogenous sisterhood of resistance with or among white women. And because all white women benefit from the system of white supremacy, antiracist white women must make their cross-racial alliances crystal clear. Because all white women are complicit in the structural determinants of white privilege, we must take every opportunity to challenge it, and therefore ourselves. Racism must be abolished and white women must not fear what this will mean.

This means listening to and thinking with women of color very carefully. If I do not feel unsettled, I am not listening. If I am not destabilized about my place in the scheme of things, I am not doing the work. I must never remain silent in a moment of injustice; it is my responsibility to engage the difficulties of racism before any person of color does. Never think that color does not matter. Never be afraid or believe that you cannot stand against injustice. Absolutely do not remain silent because you are frightened to make a mistake. Risk everything and the support you need comes forth.

As a white antiracist feminist, I am determined to fight to abolish all forms of degradation of the earth and its people. This means that I must do everything I can to demand the end of misogynoir capitalist patriarchy and make things as uncomfortable as possible for the white women who continue to support it.

There is only the sisterhood we build, in and under the skin. There are racist and sexist and class fissures to abolish. If there is a united sisterhood at present, it is among Black women voters who continuously vote against misogynoir in huge and massive numbers. So follow them and at least vote like a Black woman.

To conclude: There is a rare possibility today of an expansive new anti-racist feminist working class. If it materializes it will be made up of mainly women but also all genders, races in differing locations of labor— including striking teachers in West Virginia, Oklahoma, Arizona, and California, and Greece and Argentina; TSA workers; restaurant workers; air traffic controllers: domestic workers; flight attendants and Google workers. This organizing must be mobile and reparative and restorative. I want to keep marching, risking, wondering, striking, and connecting toward this #Feminism4the99.

The writer Tayari Jones says there is no "halfway between moral and immoral," that "justice seldom dwells in the middle." The middle is not where antiracist white women need to be. We need to be extremists against any form of white privilege, most especially when it is used in the service of misogyny, climate denial, xenophobia, nationalism, and human suffering. Risk everything to do so.

ACKNOWLEDGMENTS

This short book is part of my life project of political writing and activism. It often shortcuts much of the process of its *becoming* because it is the only way for me to write in this moment. I move forward from here with some very old thoughts but hopefully in new ways. Please see my web site, http://zillaheisenstein.wordpress.com, to view the many books and articles that are the foundation of this discussion. It is in these books and articles that you can find a full accounting of my intellectual debts as well as the huge communities of writers and activists that have made my political life possible. Thank you to each and every person.

Tamura Lomax and Monica Casper, editors of *The Feminist Wire* have been extraordinary feminist colleagues and comrades who often published earlier iterations of writing found here. As such, they have been an integral part of my thinking in these last several years.

Thanks to Gioconda Herrara of the Gender Studies Program of FLACSO (Facultad Latinoamericana de Ciencias Sociales) and the women in Quito, Ecuador, for inviting me to speak with them about the 2016 presidential election. And thanks to Anju Manikoth, Meena Menon, and Tejaswini Madabhushi of the Urban Action School in Hyderabad, India, for hosting me there, and P. K. Das and Tilu Bal Das in Mumbai. The meetings and discussions comparing Trump and Modi on nationalism and feminism were formative for me.

I am indebted to my hosts Miyuki Daimaruya and Mariko Adachi for time spent at the Gender Studies Program at Ochanomizu University in Tokyo. I am also grateful to meetings and conversations in Hiroshima with antimilitarist feminists. My visit with Mina Watanabe, who directs the Women's Active Museum on War and Peace (WAM) and who has navigated reparations for sexual crimes against the so-called comfort women of the Second World War, had a deep impact on my understanding of sexual violence and imperial power.

Meetings and conversations hosted by Alexander Kondakov with gay activists in St. Petersburg, Russia, were invaluable to my understanding of Putin's homophobic misogynist nationalism.

Much of the writing here describes my political involvement leading up to the 2016 election and working in the resistance after. This includes my activity with the African American Policy Forum, One Billion Ris-

ing, #SayHerName, #International Women's Strike, and
#Feminism4the99. My work with One Billion Rising
clarified for me the need to rewrite our understanding
of justice and revolution by placing sex violence at the
core. Working with Eve Ensler, Kim Crenshaw, Laura
Flanders, Susan Celia Swan, Beverly Guy Sheftall, Tithi
Bhattacharya, Barbara Smith, and Cinzia Arruzza has
once again given the term *comrade* new meaning. Meeting and getting to know Michelle Alexander, Winona
LaDuke, Eddie Glaude, Rosa Clemente, Dara Baldwin,
Naomi Klein, and Phyllis Bennis, to name a few, at the
Stone Ridge gathering *almost* makes up for the election
of Trump.

I want to thank my "thought" friends on Facebook,
some of whom I have yet to meet in person, and tell
them how much I appreciate them. I log on because I
look forward to seeing what you say and think. I often
get ideas for what to read from your postings. So you are
present here whether you have any sense of this or not.
Thank you, Imani Perry, Salamishah Tillet, Brittney Cooper, Darnell Moore, Tamura Lomax, Lisa Duggan, Sarah
Schulman, Janell Hobson, Minnie Bruce Pratt, Aishah
Shahidah Simmons, and Keeanga-Yamahtta Taylor.

I am so fortunate to have lifelong loving political
friends who are always ready to listen and to read my
early thoughts as they first meander and take shape.
These friends are continually generous as I struggle to

unravel my ideas and search for clarity. I have come to cherish their specialness in meeting me where I am, whether they are fully available or not. They never ask me to be quiet or say they do not have time, even when everyone, including myself, would prefer to not think about what is happening in the moment. Thank you to Ellen Wade, Maureen Brodoff, Rebecca Riley, and Rosalind Petchesky, and Chandra Mohanty, who have been present for a lifetime.

My comrades at Ithaca College, where I taught for forty years, remain a vital part of my intellectual political life. Thank you Patricia Zimmermann, Naeem Inayatulluh, Mary Bentley, Asma Barlas, Tom Shevory, Tanya Saunders, and Peyi Soyinka for continuing to be a source of nurture and innovation for me.

I thank my artist friend Barbara Mink for our long walks and talks as I searched through my mind while writing this. I also thank her for many edits. Thank you to Jeff Claus and Judy Hyman for the music they write and also for their encouragement for me to write. Thanks to Sandra Greene, who I first met when we both spoke on a panel about the Rodney King beating, and who always lets me teeter at the edge. Carole Boyce Davies very often lightens my spirit as we talk over lunch. Janet Haskell's friendship buoys my spirit when I cannot do so alone. Toni House clears the way at home for me to have precious time. Thank you Sital Kalantry, a kindred feminist and legal mind, for meals with the boys and Eduardo's pizzas. Thanks to Susan Buck-Morss for so often thinking about similar issues, and with me.

Working with Nia Michelle Nunn and Nydia Blas reminds me always of fabulous young Black women's brilliance. I have become devoted to Ithaca's Southside Community Center through them. My work in Decarcerate Tompkins County reminds me always to think about those who are caged. Paula Ionide has been extraordinary in helping me know the importance of this work. And I am lucky enough to live on the same street as my sister-comrade Chandra Talpade Mohanty. We share conversations of friendship and politics that constantly nurture me.

Thanks to my friends Angela Davis and Gina Dent. Every time we hike together I become more of an abolitionist. Hiking and exploring Yosemite sealed the deal.

My most incredible debt for assisting me with this book is to Miriam Brody, a writer herself, and my dearest friend in all things. She has read and commented on every single word I have ever written for my entire life. When I was reluctant to take on this book and was trying to decide whether to do so, she read the first ten pages for me and said, you must write this. So I did. But she deserves no blame.

My daughter, Sarah Eisenstein Stumbar, shares everything about my life. She always listens and helps me think about this world in newly urgent ways. As a social medicine doctor committed to the health care of every human being, with sexual health rights at the forefront of her life, and active in #WhiteCoatsForBlackLives, she lets me hope and believe. My optimism is sourced from her.

And almost last, but absolutely not least, is Richard Stumbar, the father of Sarah and my life partner and insurgent attorney. He is by my side through all things. He has read and commented on the book with his cautious eye. He listens at all times of day and night. I have come to think I must be impossible to live with, but he assures me I am not.

And, last, but also first, is the team at Monthly Review Press that assisted with this book. I thank Gloria Jacobs, my copy editor. She edited my manuscript with her brilliant skill: clarifying my voice while never erasing it. She continually asked for more clarity, more examples, more preciseness. To whatever degree I have achieved this, it is due to her incredible generous labor.

My further thanks to Susie Day, Martin Paddio, and Jamil Jonna who graciously used their time to assist with publication. And special thanks to Namaah Kumar for her beautiful image for the book cover. Finally, my deep gratitude to Michael Yates, editor at Monthly Review Press, for his editorial assist while often differing with my view of things. He helps nourish my belief that we can build camaraderie across differences.

I know I will think of so many more people that should be named and thanked. I apologize in advance for my oversights, but please know that if you are or have been a part of my life and work, I am thanking you, always.

SELECTED READINGS

BOOKS

Alexander, Michelle. *The New Jim Crow: Mass Incarceration in the Age of Colorblindness*. New York: The New Press, 2010.

Alcoff, Linda Martin. *The Future of Whiteness*. Malden, MA: Polity, 2015.

Ambedkar, B.R. *Annihilation of Caste*. London: Verso Books, 2016.

Anderson, Carol. *White Rage: The Unspoken Truth of Our Racial Divide*. New York: Bloomsbury, 2016.

Bullard, Robert D. and Beverly Wright. *The Wrong Complexion for Protection: How the Government Response to Disaster Endangers African American Communities*. New York: New York University Press, 2012.

Burton, Susan and Cari Lynn. *Becoming Ms. Burton: From Prison to Recovery to Leading the Fight for Incarcerated Women*. New York: The New Press, 2017.

Clausewitz, Carl von. *On War*. Edited by Michael Howard and Peter Paret. Princeton: Princeton University Press, 1976.

Coates, Ta-Nehisi. *Between the World and Me*. New York: Penguin, 2015.

_____. *We Were Eight Years in Power*. New York: Penguin, 2017.

Davis, Angela. *Women, Race, and Class*. New York: Vintage, 1983.

_____. *Are Prisons Obsolete?* New York: Seven Stories Press, 2003.

Desmond, Matthew. *Evicted: Poverty and Profit in the American City*. New York: Broadway Books, 2016.

Eisenstein, Zillah, ed. *Capitalist Patriarchy and the Case for Socialist Feminism*. New York: Monthly Review Press, 1979.

Feimster, Crystal N. *Southern Horrors: Women and the Politics of Rape and Lynching*. Cambridge: Harvard University Press, 2011.

Feinberg, Leslie. *Stone Butch Blues: A Novel*. Ithaca: Firebrand Books, 1993.

Gay, Roxane. *Hunger: A Memoir of (My) Body*. New York: Harper Collins, 2017.

Gilligan, James. *Violence: Reflections on a National Epidemic*. New York: Vintage, 1997.

Gilmore, Ruth Wilson. *Golden Gulag: Prisons, Surplus, Crisis, and Opposition in Globalizing California*. Berkeley: University of California Press, 2007.

Glaude Jr., Eddie S. *Democracy in Black: How Race Still Enslaves the American Soul*. New York: Crown, 2016.

Gordon-Reed, Annette. *The Hemingses of Monticello: An American Family*. New York: W.W. Norton, 2008.

Hartman, Saidiya. *Lose Your Mother: A Journey Along the Atlantic Slave Route*. New York: Farrar, Straus, and Giroux, 2007.

Hidayatullah, Aysha. *Feminist Edges of the Qur'An*. New York: Oxford University Press, 2014.

Hochschild, Arlie Russell. *Strangers in Their Own Land: Anger and Mourning on the American Right*. New York: The New Press, 2016.

Hunter, Tera. *Bound in Wedlock: Slave and Free Black Marriage in the Nineteenth Century*. Cambridge: Harvard University Press, 2017.

Klein, Naomi. *No Is Not Enough: Resisting Trump's Shock Politics and Winning the World We Need*. Chicago: Haymarket Books, 2017.

Lorde, Audre. *Sister Outsider: Essays and Speeches*. Berkeley, CA: Crossing Press, 1984.

Luxemburg, Rosa. *Reform or Revolution*. Dover Books, 2006.

Piketty, Thomas. *Capital in the Twenty-First Century*. Cambridge: Harvard University Press, 2014.

Pratt, Minnie Bruce. *Walking Back Up Depot Street: Poems*. Pittsburgh: University of Pittsburgh Press, 1999.

Richie, Beth E. *Arrested Justice: Black Women, Violence, and America's Prison Nation*. New York: New York University Press, 2012.

Schwartz, Marie Jenkins. *Ties That Bound: Founding First Ladies and Slaves*. Chicago: University of Chicago Press, 2017.

Segrest, Mab. *Memoir of a Race Traitor*. Boston: South End Press, 1999.

Smith, Mychal Denzel. *Invisible Man, Got the Whole World Watching: A Young Black Man's Education*. New York: Nation Books, 2016.

Stevenson, Bryan. *Just Mercy: A Story of Justice and Redemption*. New York: Penguin, 2014.

Taylor, Keeanga-Yamahtta. *From #BlackLivesMatter to Black Liberation*. Chicago: Haymarket Books, 2016.

Tillet, Salamishah. *Sites of Slavery: Citizenship and Racial Democracy in the Post-Civil Rights Imagination*. Durham: Duke University Press, 2012.

Wekker, Gloria. *White Innocence: Paradoxes of Colonialism and Race*. Durham: Duke University Press, 2016.

Wilderson, Frank. *Incognegro: A Memoir of Exile and Apartheid*. Boston: South End Press, 2008.

Yeung, Bernice. *In a Day's Work: The Fight to End Sexual Violence Against America's Most Vulnerable Workers*. New York: The New Press, 2018.

ARTICLES

Cobb, Jelani. "William Barber Takes on Poverty and Race in the Age of Trump." *The New Yorker,* May 14, 2018.

Cooper, Brittney. "This is America's Religion of Violence: The Impunity of Police Violence & the Destruction of Sandra Bland." *Salon.com,* December 23, 2015. https://www.salon.com/2015/12/23/the_deadly_theology_that_killed_sandra_bland_inside_americas_religious_devotion_to_state_violence/.

Crenshaw, Kimberlé Williams. "The Girls Obama Forgot." *New York Times,* July 29, 2014. https://www.nytimes.com/2014/07/30/

opinion/Kimberl-Williams-Crenshaw-My-Brothers-Keeper-
Ignores-Young-Black-Women.html?ref=opinion&_r=0.

Davis, Angela. "Reflections on the Black Woman's Role in the
Community of Slaves." *The Massachusetts Review* 13, no. 1/2
(Winter-Spring, 1972): 81-100.

Garza, Alicia. "Our Cynicism Will Not Build a Movement.
Collaboration Will." *Mic,* January 26, 2017. https://mic.com/
articles/166720/blm-co-founder-protesting-isnt-about-
ho-can-be-the-most-radical-its-about-winning#.
msnpfr7mJ.

Gonnerman, Jennifer. "Before the Law." *The New Yorker,* October
6, 2014. https://www.newyorker.com/magazine/2014/10/06/
before-the-law.

_____. "Kalief Browder, 1993–2015." *The New Yorker,* June 7,
2015. http://www.newyorker.com/news/news-desk/kalief-
browder-1993-2015.

Gorelova, Anastasia. "Pussy Riot Member to Be Moved to Another
Jail after Hunger Strike." Reuters.com, October 18, 2013.
https://www.reuters.com/article/us-russia-pussyriot/pussy-
riot-member-to-be-moved-to-another-jail-after-hunger-
strike-idUSBRE99H05M20131018.

"James Baldwin: How to Cool It: Read the 1968 Landmark Q & A
on Race in America." *Esquire.* http://www.esquire.com/news-
politics/a23960/james-baldwin-cool-it/.

Jones, Tayari. "There's Nothing Virtuous About Finding Common
Ground." *Time,* November 5, 2018. http://time.com/5434381/
tayari-jones-moral-middle-.

Lartey, Jamiles. "Median Wealth of Black Americans 'Will Fall to
Zero by 2053,' Warns New Report." *The Guardian,* September
13, 2017. https://www.theguardian.com/inequality/2017/
sep/13/median-wealth-of-black-americans-will-fall-to-zero-
by-2053-warns-new-report.

Lomax, Tamura. "#SayHerName: #SandraBland Is Sojourner Truth,
Harriet Tubman, and Fannie Lou Hamer." *The Feminist Wire,*
July 22, 2015. https://www.thefeministwire.com/2015/07/

sayhername-sandrabland-is-sojourner-truth-harriet-tubman-and-fannie-lou-hamer-2/.

McBride, Michael, Traci Blackmon, Frank Reid, and Barbara Williams Skinner. "Waiting for a Perfect Protest?" *New York Times,* September 1, 2017.

Moya, Paula. "New Terms of Resistance: A Response to Zenzele Isoke." *Souls: A Critical Journal of Black Politics, Culture, and Society* 15, no. 4, (2013): 341–343.

Mueller, Mark. "See Who's Speaking at the Women's March on Washington Saturday." NJ.com, January 20, 2017. http://www.nj.com/news/index.ssf/2017/01/see_whos_speaking_at_the_womens_march_on_washingto.html.

Pleasant, Liz. "Meet the Woman Behind #BlackLivesMatter—The Hashtag That Became a Civil Rights Movement." *YES! Magazine,* Summer 2015. https://billmoyers.com/2015/05/04/meet-woman-behind-blacklivesmatter-hashtag-became-civil-rights-movement/?utm_source=General+Interest&utm_campaign=c7a89a47d3-Midweek12171412_17_2014&utm_medium=email&utm_term=0_4ebbe6839f-c7a89a47d3-168294985.

Pollitt, Katha. "The Women's March Succeeded Because It Spoke to Women's Outrage." *The Nation,* January 23, 2017. https://www.thenation.com/article/the-womens-march-succeeded-because-it-spoke-to-womens-outrage/.

Pope Francis. "Evangelii Gaudium." *Libreria Editrice Vaticana.* http://www.vatican.va/holy_father/francesco/apost_exhortations/documents/papa-francesco_esortazione-ap_20131124_evangelii-gaudium_en.htm.

Rich, Frank. "In Conversation: Chris Rock: What's Killing Comedy. What's Saving America." *New York Magazine,* December 1, 2014. https://www.vulture.com/2014/11/chris-rock-frank-rich-in-conversation.html.

Smarsh, Sarah. "Liberal Blind Spots Are Hiding the Truth About 'Trump Country.'" *New York Times,* July 19, 2018.

Spillers, Hortense. "Mama's Baby, Papa's Maybe: An American Grammar Book." *Diacritics* 17, no. 2, Culture and

Countermemory: The "American" Connection (Summer 1987): 64–81.

Stein, Perry and Sandhya Somashekhar. "It Started with a Retiree. Now the Women's March Could Be the Biggest Inauguration Demonstration," January 3, 2017. ttps://www.washingtonpost. com/national/it-started-with-a-grandmother-in-hawaii- now-the-womens-march-on-washington-is-poised-to-be- the-biggest-inauguration-demonstration/2017/01/03/8af6- 1686-c6e2-11e6-bf4b-2c064d32a4bf_story. html?noredirect=on&utm_term=.011af025fd93.

Wells, Veronica. "'I'm Ready . . . This Means War' Sandra Bland's Mother Eulogizes Daughter, Prepares to Fight for Justice." MadameNoire, July 22, 2015. http://madamenoire. com/549162/im-readythis-means-war-sandra-blands-mother- eulogizes-daughter-prepares-to-fight-for-justice/.

SELECTED ONLINE MATERIAL

African American Intellectual History Society (AAIHS). "Remem- bering Sandra Bland." Online forum, July 9-13, 2018.   https:// www.aaihs.org/online-forum-remembering-sandra-bland/.

African American Policy Forum. "Reclaiming Racial Justice for Us All: Women of Color Speak Out on MBK." http://www.aapf. org/recent/2014/07/mbk-webinar-woc.

Democracy Now. "'Running While Black:' Protests Swell over Death of Freddie Gray in Baltimore Police Custody." April 23, 2015. https://www.youtube.com/watch?v=Amno2Ukn_k0.

The Equal Justice Initiative (EJI) exhibition on Lynching at the Brooklyn Museum. https://eji.org/news/lynching-in-america- exhibit-opens-at-brooklyn-museum.

Human Rights Watch: "Domestic Workers." http://www.hrw.org/ topic/womens-rights/domestic-workers.

Mammablack. "On January 21, 2017, Black Women' s Blueprint Will March on Washington." Posted January 6, 2017. http://www. mamablack.org/single-post/2017/01/06/On-January-21-2017- Black-Women's-Blueprint-Will-March-on-Washington.

Two Hundred Black Men draft letter on Behalf of their Sisters. http://aapf.org/2014/05/an-open-letter-to-president-obama/.

Women of color draft letter supporting the letter by men of color critiquing My Brother's Keeper. https://docs.google.com/document/d/1jTDygnRPVdl1YBEAGaouoNdhX2fi42qOEePIcARN_LE/pub.

World Health Organization. "Gender, Equity, and Human Rights." www.who.int/gender/violence/who_multicountry_study/en/.

WEBSITES

Cosecha Movement: http://www.lahuelga.com/#daca-header.

Dream Defenders: http://www.dreamdefenders.org.

Hands Up United: http://www.handsupunited.org.

International Women's Strike: https://www.womenstrikeus.org.

Million Hoodies: http://millionhoodies.net.

Movement for Black Lives: https://m4bl.org./

National Domestic Workers Alliance: https://www.domesticworkers.org.

NEWW: Network of East-West Women: https://www.neww.org/.

Occupy Wall Street: http://occupywallst.org.

One Billion Rising (OBR): https://www.onebillionrising.org.

Project South: https://projectsouth.org.

Say Her Name: http://www.aapf.org/shn-campaign/.

FILM

Burns, Ken and Sarah Burns, directors. *The Central Park Five*. 2012; Florentine Films in association with WETA. http://www.imdb.com/title/tt2380247/. NOTE: The following PBS website has a link to view film: https://www.kanopy.com/product/ken-burns-central-park-five.

CD

Shigematsu, Setsu, Cameron Granadino, and Jolie Chea. *Visions of Abolition: From Critical Resistance to a New Way of Life*. https://www.visionsofabolition.org/.

NEWLY SELECTED READINGS SINCE THE CONCLUSION OF MY WRITING BUT WONDERFULLY RELEVANT TO MANY CONVERSATIONS

Arceneaux, Michael. *I Can't Date Jesus: Love, Sex, Family, Race, and Other Reasons I've Put My Faith in Beyoncé.* New York: Atria, 2018.

Carruthers, Charlene A. *Unapologetic: A Black, Queer, and Feminist Mandate for Radical Movements.* Boston: Beacon Press, 2018.

Cooper, Brittney. *Eloquent Rage: A Black Feminist Discovers Her Superpower.* New York: St. Martin's Press, 2018.

Khan-Cullors, Patrisse and Asha Bandele. *When They Call You a Terrorist: A Black Lives Matter Memoir.* New York: St. Martin's Press, 2018.

Lomax, Tamura. *Jezebel Unhinged: Loosing the Black Female Body in Religion and Culture.* Durham: Duke University Press, 2018.

Moore, Darnell. *No Ashes in the Fire: Coming of Age Black and Free in America.* Nation Books, New York, 2018.

Perry, Imani. *Looking for Lorraine: The Radiant and Radical Life of Lorraine Hansberry.* Boston: Beacon Press, 2018.

_____. *Vexy Thing: On Gender and Liberation.* Durham: Duke University Press, 2018.

Ransby, Barbara. *Making All Black Lives Matter: Reimagining Freedom in the Twenty-First Century.* Oakland: University of California Press, 2018.

Smarsh, Sarah. *Heartland: A Memoir of Working Hard and Being Broke in the Richest Country on Earth.* New York: Scribner, 2018.

Traister, Rebecca. *Good and Mad: The Revolutionary Power of Women's Anger.* New York: Simon & Schuster, 2018.